WOMAN AS IMAGE
IN
MEDIEVAL LITERATURE

Woman As Image
In Medieval Literature

FROM THE TWELFTH CENTURY TO DANTE

Joan M. Ferrante

THE LABYRINTH PRESS
Durham, North Carolina

Library of Congress Cataloging in Publication Data

Ferrante, Joan M., 1936-
  Woman as image in medieval literature from the
twelfth century to Dante.

  Reprint. Originally published: Columbia University
Press, 1975.
  Includes index.
  1. Literature, Medieval—History and criticism.
2. Women in literature. I. Title.
PN682.W6F4 1985   809′.93352042   84-29689
ISBN 0-939464-43-8

Library of Congress CIP Data

Printed in the United States of America

for Carolyn Heilbrun

Così andammo infino a la lumera,
parlando cose che 'l tacere è bello,
sì com'era 'l parlar colà dov'era.

Contents

WOMAN AS IMAGE
IN
MEDIEVAL LITERATURE

Introduction

One of the more striking features of twelfth century literature is the importance of female characters. They are not portrayed as "real people" with human problems; they are symbols, aspects of philosophical and psychological problems that trouble the male world. In the Latin allegories, women personify cosmological forces that govern man's life; in lyric and romance, they represent his ideals, his aspirations, the values of his society. But the embodiment of these forces and values in female figures is significant. The fictional world in which the twelfth-century hero moves is dominated, for good or ill, by women. The aim of this study is to analyze the symbolic treatment of women in the literature of the high Middle Ages, from the twelfth century to Dante, tracing a development, where appropriate, from religious and secular works of earlier periods. Only those genres which are essentially symbolic will be considered—exegesis, allegory, lyric, and romance.[1]

From the vast body of medieval exegesis, I have selected certain areas that seem most pertinent to the symbolism of women: the meanings ascribed to "historical" figures, particularly Eve, and the interpretation of the bride in the Song of Songs. There are two opposing views of woman in medieval exegesis, and the negative view is the one most frequently met. With an astonishing consistency, biblical women, if they are good or potentially redeemable, are said to represent the church; if bad, they stand for the lower or weaker parts of

[1] I am using "symbolic" to denote any genre in which a meaning other than the literal is suggested by the text.

man, for carnal desires, or inconstancy of mind.[2] Woman, as the most obvious object of male concupiscence, is made to represent lust and thus is held responsible for it; the object of temptation becomes the cause. And because heresy, like woman, attracts with superficial beauty, woman is also identified with heresy—indeed, the love of woman can itself be a form of idolatry. Yet, in the Song of Songs, the groom's love for his bride represents the love of God for his church; their union stands for the union of God and man. In this case, the woman represents that part of mankind that will be saved.

In the allegorical tradition, which is more classical than religious in origin, the positive symbolism of women is much stronger; this is the result of two separate strains—one philosophical, the other rhetorical. The Neo-Platonic descriptions of creation as the union of opposing elements—of male and female forces—evokes a more positive view of marriage and of woman, for marriage is the principle of unity in the individual and in the cosmos; order in the universe cannot be preserved without the cooperation of female elements and female animals. The rhetorical tradition provides the personification in female figures of abstract concepts which are essential to man's moral and intellectual well-being—the virtues, the liberal arts, philosophy. In the battle between vices and virtues, which is central to Christian morality, both groups are female; inner conflict is seen in terms of women pulling in opposite directions, towards good or evil. In a psychomachia, man sees both his lower and his higher impulses as women.

This double view is reflected in courtly literature, which is concerned to a great extent with the investigation of man's emotions and impulses. The lady represents the force of love—she may even be confused with Love, particularly in the lyric. Love awakens man to a new sense of himself, to higher aspirations, but sometimes he is drawn away from his love by worldly desires, which, in romance, are often represented by other women. When and if he overcomes his lower im-

---

[2] These two poles are often juxtaposed in what Guldan calls the Eve-Mary antithesis; for a detailed study of the connection between Eve and Mary in medieval art see E. Guldan, *Eva und Maria, Eine Antithese als Bildmotiv* (Graz/Köln: Böhlaus, 1966).

pulses, he is reunited with the woman he loves and that union signifies the harmony he has achieved within himself and with his world. This kind of moral and social harmony is sought in courtly literature in the twelfth and early thirteenth centuries, when it is a goal men can believe in and aspire to. Later in the thirteenth century individual problems are resolved only outside of society; the romance quest becomes a religious quest, a personal one, which can be achieved only when the individual alienates himself from his society. With the rejection of the courtly ethic, the symbolic status of woman also suffers; she becomes a temptation rather than an inspiration. As the social world of chivalry dissolves, the microcosm begins to disintegrate as well. Even in allegory, and to a lesser extent in lyric, during the later period the emphasis is on the fragmentation of the psyche, not on harmony. Thirteenth-century literature shows the strong influence of two anti-feminist views: the Aristotelian—of woman as a defective male, a creature lacking in reason, useful only to bear children; and the moralist—of woman as a threat to man's salvation. Only in lyric poetry and in mystic writings, where love is the major theme, does woman remain a force for good. But she is no longer a symbol of something in man; she has become a separate entity—an angel or star, or the Virgin Mary—in other words, an intermediary between man and God. Man's goal is not union with her, but union with God through her.

Dante picks up all the strains of the earlier traditions and brings them together—the positive and negative symbols, the historical figures as exempla and the personified abstractions, the love of man and woman as a figure for and step towards the union of man and God. Dante's world is fragmented; his Hell reveals the isolation in which men live, and Dante himself writes the comedy in exile from his native society. But he yearns for harmony, and the harmony he presents as the ideal for himself and all mankind is possible only through women. Dante can see good as well as bad aspects of himself as female; he can even see a feminine side of God, in the trinity of Mary, Beatrice, and Lucy, and in the identification of Beatrice with Christ.

The ability to accept and even encourage the feminine side of human nature is characteristic of Dante and of much twelfth-century literature, but not of thirteenth-century thought.[3] In this, as in his concept of empire, Dante is still attached to an ideal which has lost its force if not its validity.

The fusion of male and female characteristics is illustrated by a confusion of male and female characters in literature and in art. The ideals of male and female beauty in the high Middle Ages seem to have been quite similar:[4] a hero can be mistaken for or exchange roles with a heroine; sculpted and painted angels can be seen as male or female.[5] Wisdom (*Sapientia*), sometimes interchangeable with Philosophy, may appear either as a woman or, less frequently, as Christ, the *Logos;* sometimes Christ is pictured with the inscription *Sancta Sophia,* a feminine title.[6] The Virgin Mary is often portrayed in the

---

[3] I was alerted to the importance of the blending of male and female characteristics in literature by C. G. Heilbrun's *Toward a Recognition of Androgyny* (New York: Knopf, 1973), a book which played no small part in arousing my interest in this subject and to whose thesis I hope this study offers added support.

[4] See A. M. Colby, *The Portrait in Twelfth-Century Literature: An Example of the Stylistic Originality of Chrétien de Troyes* (Genève: Droz, 1965), which analyzes in detail descriptions of men and women in medieval French romances. The heroes are young, beardless men, similar in coloring and feature to the heroines; the same parts of the body are praised (with the exception of the woman's breasts, which are, however, not always included).

[5] See J. Villette, *L'Ange dans l'Art d'Occident du XII–XVIᵉ Siècle* (Paris: H. Laurens, 1940). In the early Middle Ages, Villette says, angels were shown mostly as adolescent males; in the tenth and eleventh centuries, the female type became more frequent and female traits predominated even in warrior angels until the thirteenth century, when a kind of neutral figure took over, presumably a return to the adolescent male.

[6] A. N. Didron, *Christian Iconography* (London: George Bell, 1886, 1891), Vol. I, p. 179, describes an early twelfth-century illumination of God, young and lightly bearded, giving life to the sciences under the inscription Sancta Sophia; M. T. d'Alverny, "La Sagesse et ses Sept Filles," *Mélanges dédiés à la mémoire de Félix Grat* (Paris: Pecquer-Grat, 1946), Vol. I, p. 266, describes a similar illumination. Herrad of Landsberg, in an illustration of the capture of Leviathan, a variation of the genealogical tree, depicts Christ on the cross as young, beardless, crowned, and robed, looking very much like a woman, as if consciously to create confusion between Christ and

twelfth century (less frequently in the thirteenth) as the throne of wisdom (*sedes sapientiae*), with Christ (wisdom) on her lap. In such statues, Forsyth comments, the majesty of male and female figures is combined; "the male and female provinces interlock as do the figures." [7] Christ is both the *Logos* of the New Testament (masculine) and the Wisdom of the Old Testament (feminine). Another Greek term is sometimes used for the divine attribute of wisdom, the feminine *Nous,* which appears in the cosmological allegories of the twelfth century as a female figure who receives God's command and translates it into existence. [8] *Anima mundi* is another figure of sexual ambiguity; an unorthodox concept at best, the neo-Platonic World Soul, always female, was sometimes identified with the Holy Spirit, normally male. [9] To compound the confusion, D'Alverny has identified an illumination of *Anima mundi* in a twelfth century manuscript as a variation of the human microcosmos figure, usually shown as a man and occasionally as Christ. [10]

Obviously one part of the problem is language—the gender of the nouns involved. To a great extent, the gender of an abstract noun determines the gender of the personification, but that is not the end of

---

Mary, who would normally appear in such a genealogy; see *Hortus deliciarum,* ed. Jos. Walter (Strasbourg/Paris: Le Roux, 1952), pl. xvi.

[7] I. H. Forsyth, *The Throne of Wisdom, Wood Sculptures of the Madonna in Romanesque France* (Princeton: Princeton University Press, 1972), p. 29. Cf. A. Fletcher, *Allegory, the Theory of a Symbolic Mode* (Ithaca: Cornell University Press, 1964), p. 356: allegorical heroes, personifications, are not men and women but divided androgynes.

[8] According to d'Alverny, "Le Cosmos Symbolique du XIIe Siècle," *AHDL* 28 (1953), 51, the Greeks distinguished *nous,* pure intelligence, which determines the motion of celestial essences, from *logos,* reason that moves the human spirit. Christ would thus be *Logos* in his human incarnation, *Nous* as the second person of the trinity.

[9] See Guillaume de Conches, *De philosophia mundi,* I, xv (in PL 172, erroneously ascribed to Honorius). This identification of the *Anima mundi* with the Holy Spirit is the center of major twelfth-century controversies involving Abelard and Guillaume on one side, Bernard of Clairvaux and Guillaume de St.-Thierry on the other; see T. Gregory, *Anima Mundi, La Filosofia di Guglielmo di Conches e la Scuola di Chartres* (Firenze: Sansoni, 1955), pp. 106–21.

[10] Cosmos, pp. 74 and 79.

it. Since, in the early and high Middle Ages, ideas were believed to have an existence of their own, the symbol was closely identified with the thing symbolized.[11] The fact that a human quality or a divine attribute was represented as a woman meant that it must have female characteristics like giving birth or milk, that there was something essentially female about it. And this in turn might encourage a better attitude towards the human female or at least towards woman as a symbol. At the same time, of course, words can operate the other way. It is built into medieval language, hence into medieval thought, that women are connected with matter because they give birth: the word mother, *mater,* contains in it the root of matter, *materia.* The word virtue, *virtus,* is connected not only with *vis,* strength, but with *vir,* man:

> Vir nuncupatus, quia maior in eo vis est quam in feminis: unde et virtus nomen accepit. ... Mulier vero a mollitie ... ideo virtus maxima viri, mulieris minor.
>
> [Isidore, *Etymologiae,* XI, ii, 17–19] [12]
>
> He is called "man" because there is greater "strength" in him than in women: whence "virtue" takes its name. . . . But "woman" comes from "softness" . . . therefore there is greater virtue in man and less in woman.

Other, also supposedly scientific, beliefs contributed to such attitudes. The physiological theories of sex reveal how deeply the moral prejudices went: woman was held to be more given to lust than man because she was thought to be, in her humors, more cold and wet. This is explained in various ways: according to Adelard of Bath, the humidity in woman causes desire; the cold keeps blood from being

---

[11] The reality of ideas is the basic tenet of Realism, as opposed to Nominalism, a major issue in twelfth- and thirteenth-century philosophical debate. The force and extent of symbolism can be seen in most biblical exegesis; see Chapter I. It is discussed by Edgar de Bruyne in *Études d'esthétique médiévale,* 3 vol. (Brussels: De Tempel, 1946) and by M.-D. Chenu, *La Théologie au douzième siècle,* Etudes de philosophie médiévale, 45 (Paris: Librairie Philosophique Vrin, 1966).

[12] *Isidori Hispalensis Episcopi, Etymologiarum sive Originum,* Libri XX, ed. W. M. Lindsay (1911; repr. Oxford: Clarendon, 1957, 1962).

digested, so the blood must be purged through coitus (seed is con-
verted blood).[13] The coldness can have the further effect of incubating
disease: a woman who has slept with a leper will not contract the
disease herself because it remains dormant in her cold body, but when
it encounters the warmth of another man, it comes to life and infects
him (*Quaest. nat.*, 41). Guillaume de Conches presents similar explanations: since a woman is cold and wet, the fire is harder to start but
burns longer.[14] Guillaume insists that the woman produces a seed
towards the conception of a child just as the man does, the proof for
which lies in the fact that boys inherit traits, primarily weaknesses,
from their mothers.[15] It is not true, he insists, that the male seed will
suffice, not even in rape (the idea being that the will must consent for
seed to be emitted), because although the woman may be unwilling at
first, the weakness of the flesh will prevail and desire, hence seed, will
follow. The matrix of the woman, according to Guillaume, is formed
like a casket or vase, with a wide mouth at the top, a round belly
below, and a long neck in between. Inside, the surface is hairy in
order to retain the seed, and it has cells imprinted like money with the
human figure; in prostitutes, however, the hairs that should hold the
seed are soiled or covered, from the frequency of coitus and so, like
oiled marble, they immediately reject the seed and the prostitute does
not conceive.[16]

It is no wonder, then, that woman should be connected with
lust, nor that man should fear contact with her. And it is not surprising
to see the serpent pictured with a woman's head, or lust described as a

[13] *Quaestiones Naturales*, ed. M. Müller, *Beiträge sur Geschichte der Philosophie und Theologie des Mittelalters*, 31 (Münster, 1934), Q. 42. Bernard Silvester makes lust a direct result of gluttony: the digestion of food produces fluids which give strength to the body, but overeating produces excessive vapors that cause sperm, which are emitted through the genitals because that organ is just below the belly (commentary on *Aeneid*, Bk. IV).

[14] *Dragmaticon, Dialogus de Substantiis Physicis* (Strassburg: Argentorati, 1567), VI, 238–39; and *De phil. mundi*. IV, xiv.

[15] *Drag.*, VI, 242; *De phil. mundi*, IV, xii.

[16] *Drag.*, VI, 241; *De phil. mundi*, ibid., same comments on rape.

monster with the head of a virgin (for the image of desire), the body of a goat (for stinking appetite), and the back of a wolf (for the depredation of virtue).[17] Women are inevitably connected with the things of this world, with personal affections and desires, and with possessions; the more corrupt this world seems, the more dangerous woman appears. And life always offers circumstances to support prejudices, some of which are self-fulfilling, as in the connection of women with heresy. Women were often mistrusted by the church establishment for their religious fervor as well as their seductiveness, and they were rarely permitted to play important roles after the early Middle Ages. So they were drawn to sects like the Cathars, which encouraged them to take part and to preach, or to groups like the Beguines, which gave them an active function in the world, or to independent convents, which the regular monastic orders first refused to take responsibility for and later condemned for disobedience.[18] The involvement of women in such groups no doubt reinforced the identification of women with heresy.

My concern in this study is not with the historical or sociological position of women in the twelfth and thirteenth centuries, a subject that is fascinating but outside the scope of this work. I would, however, like to note that many women played important roles in the history of these periods.[19] In the early Middle Ages, women were ap-

---

[17] The monster of lust is described by Alanus de Insulis in *Summa de Arte Praedicatoria*, Ch. V (PL 210).

[18] See R. W. Southern, *Western Society and the Church in the Middle Ages* (Middlesex: Penguin Books, 1970), p. 313 ff, on the suppression of double monasteries by the Premonstratensians in the twelfth century and the refusal to admit women, and the Cistercians' neglect of nunneries and subsequent attempts to control them; see p. 319 ff, on the history of the Beguines. F. Heer, *The Medieval World, Europe 1100–1350*, trans. J. Sondheimer (New York: World Publishing, 1962), p. 264, notes that heterodox and heretic groups offered women much greater freedom than the church.

[19] Herbert Grundmann, "Die Frauen und die Literatur im Mittelalter," *Archiv für Kulturgeschichte*, 26 (1936), 129–61, discusses the importance of women in twelfth- and thirteenth-century Germany as audience and patrons of the arts, in connection with a shift from courtly to mystical literature and from social to religious concerns in life.

parently active in various areas of public life. There are numerous
examples of women who acted as regents for their husbands or sons,
women who led the defence of their towns, who conspired for power
against the rightful heirs, or who mediated between warring parties;
their exploits can be read about in contemporary histories and chroni-
cles.[20] Women continued to play a role in the high Middle Ages:
despite attempts to prevent it, women sometimes inherited fiefs for
which their husbands were permitted to discharge the military duties;
some women led armies; some even elicited high praise for their ad-
ministrative abilities.[21]

There were an astonishing number of women, particularly in
the twelfth century, who ruled lands as regents or, although rarely, as
legal heirs. Ermengarde of Narbonne inherited her father's lands and
administered them herself from 1134 to 1192. Eleanor of Aquitaine
inherited lands in the south and west of France over which she always
retained some control; she also served as regent for her second husband and two of her sons in England for short periods, and continued
to take an active part in public affairs until her death at eighty-two, in
1204. Marie and Blanche of Champagne were regents for their sons,
Marie from 1181 to 1187, and Blanche from 1201 to 1222 for an infant son born after the death of her husband; in the latter case, Marie's
claim for her son won out over the claims of her husband's sisters—a
victory for male inheritance which, ironically, left the land in the rule

---

[20] A. Lehmann, *Le rôle de la femme dans l'histoire de France au Moyen-Age* (Paris:
Berger-Levrault, 1952), cites Gregory of Tours, Einhard, Fredegar, and Frodoard for the
exploits of women in Merovingian and Carolingian France.

[21] On women inheriting fiefs, see M. Bloch, *Feudal Society,* trans. L. A. Manyon
(1961; repr. University of Chicago Press, 1968, 7th ed.), pp. 200–1; on the women who
led armies, see Lehmann, who mentions Richilde (countess of Flanders) in the eleventh
century, Ermengard of Narbonne in the twelfth, and Blanche of Champagne, Blanche of
Castile, and Beatrice (queen of Charles I) in the thirteenth; on contemporary praise, see
Lehmann, pp. 273 and 382, citing Guillaume de Jumiège, who said that Sibyl (duchess
of Normandy) did a better job as his regent than her husband had done, and Guillaume
de Tyr, who said that Mélisende, ruling her father's lands in Jerusalem for her sons,
bore a man's heart in her breast and was no less brilliant than the most brilliant prince.

of a woman for twenty-one years.[22] Jeanne of Flanders inherited her father's land and administered it while the king kept her husband in prison; her sister succeeded her in 1244. Finally, Blanche of Castile became regent of France in 1226, according to her husband's wishes, and continued to exert power until her death in 1252, even after her son's majority and despite opposition and attack. In this period, when political theory was so critical of woman's ability to reason and therefore to rule, the French barons objected from the beginning of Blanche's regency that it was not a woman's business to rule. Poems were written attacking her, saying that France was bastardized because it was under the rule of a woman. Insults were hurled at her publicly, as when she attempted to mediate between the barons and Thibaut de Champagne, in spite of which she obtained a truce among them.[23] Blanche's daughter-in-law, Marguerite, also served as regent for her son, but the attempts to circumscribe the powers of royal women became more and more frequent in the thirteenth century, and women were formally deprived of rights of succession by Phillip V (the Tall) in the early fourteenth century. French queens were no longer associated in power with their husbands as the early Capetian queens had been. The same was true in Germany: Frederic II did not name his wives in official charters as his father and grandfather had done.[24]

Though reluctant to generalize about periods, I cannot avoid drawing certain conclusions which are suggested by the literature I

[22] Lehmann, p. 310 ff.

[23] On woman's inability to rule see Thomas Aquinas, *Summa Theologica*, Suppl., Q. 19, a. 3, and Salimbene, the Franciscan chronicler, who, according to Southern [cited in *The Making of the Middle Ages* (1953, repr. New Haven: Yale University Press, 1969, 15th ed.), p. 109], lists five kinds of rule by which a man is disgraced because they are inimical to rational order—they include women, serfs, fools, boys, and enemies. As Heer points out (p. 265), there is a great discrepancy between theory and social reality in the late Middle Ages; it was common to say that women were incapable of taking part in public life, but they continued to do so. The attacks on Blanche of Castile are noted by C. Petit-Dutaillis, *The Feudal Monarchy in France and England* (1936, repr. London: Routledge and Kegan Paul, 1949), p. 292, and Lehmann, p. 340 ff.

[24] On the early queens of France, see Petit-Dutaillis, pp. 31 and 77; on later change, Lehmann, p. 218; on Frederic II, see E. Kantorowicz, *Frederick the Second*, trans. E. O. Lorimer from German, 1931 (New York: Ungar, 1967, 2nd ed.), pp. 407–8.

have studied and which seem to be supported by historical trends. The contrast between general attitudes of the twelfth century and those of the thirteenth, which is apparent in the treatment of women in literature, is supported by the views of several historians. Heer, Southern, and Cantor describe the twelfth century as a period of confident activity, of economic and intellectual expansion, and the thirteenth century as more rigid, repressive, perhaps even hysterical.[25] The decline in the positive symbolism of women in the thirteenth century is but one facet of a pervasive intellectual constraint. The confidence that Southern notes among twelfth-century thinkers in the ability to absorb and build on all that the past could offer contrasts sharply with later attempts to suppress the teaching of Aristotle's works.[26] It is true that Bernard and others fiercely attacked the ideas of Abelard and Gilbert during the twelfth century, but at the same time public debates between heretics and Catholics, and between Jews or Moslems and Christians, were not uncommon. However, the last public debate with Cathars was in 1204 and the repression of Jews began soon after: in 1215, the Fourth Lateran Council ordered Jews to wear emblems, whereas in 1179, the Third Lateran had called for toleration toward Jews; and in 1233, a papal bull forbad religious debates between Christians and Jews.[27] The Inquisition became a common feature in the thirteenth-century attack on heresy, and the Dominican order, and to some extent the Franciscan, was developed to fight heresy. In the twelfth century Peter Lombard had suggested that heretics served a function—to stimulate Christians in the search for truth. This was by no means a common belief, but it was possible in the twelfth century; the attitude of the thirteenth was to convert or destroy.

When men cling to orthodoxy and defend the status quo against attack from outside or from within, they begin to look on all identifi-

[25] Southern (*Western Society*, 275) speaks of hysteria in connection with the flagellants; general remarks about the two centuries are scattered through the works of Southern and Heer already cited, and are to be found also in N. F. Cantor, *Medieval History, The Life and Death of a Civilization* (New York: Macmillan, 1963).

[26] *Making*, p. 220.

[27] Heer, p. 115 on debates, pp. 255–56 on decrees against Jews.

able groups as suspect and dangerous. While it was possible to see some value in heresy, it was possible to see good in women as well, but as men became more frantic about the possibilities of their own salvation, they tended more and more to attack any possible threat. Heer points out that both women and Jews made positive contributions to medieval culture during what he calls the "open" period, and both were later relegated to the ghetto. He suggests that the witch-mania of the later Middle Ages, which was directed against women, was the product of "a world made schizophrenic by masculine anxieties and masculine fears." [28] The anxieties were not, themselves, ill-founded; the Pope was in virtual captivity in France, the last crusades had ended in sordid abuses, and Northern Europe was caught in an economic depression with the resultant social discontent and rebellion.

In art, insofar as one can generalize about different modes in different countries, there are similar contrasts between twelfth- and thirteenth-century works.[29] There are two shifts in form that are relevant to this study: the first is the breaking down into separate parts, which is particularly visible in architecture, as in the difference between Romanesque cathedrals (with their harmony of structure and ornament, where sculpture is part of the architectural form), and Gothic (in which the figures are isolated from their backgrounds, more like living things, but less a part of the whole).[30] The Gothic cathedrals themselves are conceived on a vast scale and, more often than not, are left unfinished. The second change is the movement away from symbolism towards a more realistic presentation of human figures and of nature. One can see this in the statues of the Virgin. Essentially a symbolic figure in Romanesque sculpture, she is often shown with an

[28] Heer, p. 254.

[29] In art, as in literature, one can always find exceptions to what are put forth as trends, nonetheless certain types do predominate in certain periods, and the generalizations are made on the basis of the prevalent types.

[30] Similarly, d'Alverny suggests, the figure of Sagesse loses importance as she produces more and more offshoots, "s'affaiblit en se dissociant" (Sagesse, p. 271), a fragmentation of a different kind.

adult Christ on her lap to signify that she is the temple of God, the throne of Wisdom, the church holding her priest. However, in Gothic art she is either the gentle mother holding a baby, the nursing mother, or the crowned queen of heaven, alongside but separate from the statue of Christ.[31] The cult of the Virgin encouraged the depiction of scenes from her life and the telling of stories about her miracles, all of which emphasized her humanity and her concern for man. Although the miracles imply great power in heaven, the presentation in literature and art is of a gentle woman. The awesome symbol of the earlier period is gone (though not entirely—it does appear in illustrations of the Apocalypse). Scenes from the Virgin's life are also used to illustrate the virtues; she becomes, in other words, an exemplum rather than a symbol. Even personifications of the virtues and vices, although they persist in the late thirteenth century, are sometimes replaced by contemporary figures, the virtues shown as nuns, vices as townswomen.[32] The move away from symbols has more effect on the presentation of women than the continued worship of the Virgin, for it is when men think of desirable qualities as female, even as female impulses in themselves, that they exalt female figures in literature. When they think of women as real beings, they tend to see them only as child-bearers, or as temptresses, and the literary possibilities are slight or negative.

[31] Forsyth, pp. 4 and 30, contrasts the Romanesque with the Gothic madonna; pp. 22–24, he discusses Mary's depiction as the church, with chasuble and pallium; see M. Delcor, *Les Vierges Romanes de Cerdagne et Conflent dans l'Histoire et dans l'Art* (Barcelona: Dalmau, 1970), p. 95, on Mary as the nursing mother. E. Mâle, *The Gothic Image*, trans. D. Nussey from French (1913; repr. New York: Dutton, 1958), p. ix, notes the same humanizing or desymbolizing of the figure of Christ on the cross, shown triumphant with a jewelled crown and open eyes in the twelfth century, with drooping body and closed eyes in the thirteenth.

[32] See A. Katzenellenbogen, *Allegories of the Virtues and Vices in Mediaeval Art*, trans. A. J. P. Crick (1939; repr. New York: Norton, 1964), p. 7. This does occur in the twelfth century but more frequently later. M. W. Bloomfield, *The Seven Deadly Sins* (1952, repr. Michigan State University Press, 1967), pp. 129–36, notes an increase in the treatment of sins after 1200, particularly in social satire, in which they may be presented as daughters of the devil and married off to different social classes.

In this study, I have concentrated on what seem to me the most interesting or influential works in a genre, with some thought to following the Latin and Romance traditions that Dante was working from. I have therefore omitted German lyric and romance, which, probably more than any others, champion the idea of mutual love. Because I was only concerned with the symbolism of women in literature, I did not consider women in epic poetry. Nor have I made a special effort to discuss women writers, with the exception of Marie de France, who is included because she reverses convention in a most intriguing way. The Provençal women who wrote lyric poetry are not mentioned because they employ the same conventions as the men. In literature before Dante, it is only women writers, as far as I know, who seem to believe that a man can inspire a woman through love in the same way a woman can inspire a man. But among women, it is only Marie de France who applies the same sort of symbolism to men as to women. Even Hildegard of Bingen, who speaks movingly of human love and asserts that man and woman can attain divinity through each other's love, makes the woman the symbol: woman is Love . . . she functions as an angel and a lodestar in the process of attaining the divine . . . her female form embodies for her love the fountain of Wisdom.[33]

When, in the chapters that follow, I discuss the fathers and later exegetes, I attempt simply to summarize or characterize their interpretations of women. In the discussion of a literary work, however, I inevitably give an interpretation which is offered not as *the* reading of the poem, but simply as a contribution towards the understanding of the work from yet another perspective. The interpretations are meant to complement, not supplant. My hope is that by bringing together the various symbolic presentations of women in the genres that rely most heavily on symbols, I might add something to an understanding of the literature. My conclusions about the two periods were not actively sought, but became harder and harder to avoid. Although one cannot

[33] From *Causae et Curae,* cited by P. Dronke, *Medieval Latin and the Rise of European Love-Lyric* (Oxford: Clarendon, 1968), Vol. I, p. 66 ff.

safely draw conclusions about life from literature, when literature bears out impressions reached on the basis of study in other areas, the conclusions may have some validity. In any case, they remain of secondary importance in this study. I would go no further than to suggest that the generally positive presentation of women in twelfth-century literature does not indicate a positive attitude towards women, but it does indicate a positive attitude towards life, while the more negative portrayal of women in the thirteenth century reveals a far more bleak view of the human condition. Dante's presentation of women, on the other hand, indicates more about him than it does about his world. It reveals a capacity to see mankind as one, to accept women as friends (guides and critics) as well as inspirations and temptations, in short, as human beings.

For the generous exchange of ideas before, during, and after the writing of this book, I am in debt beyond measure to my friends and colleagues, Professors Robert Hanning, Frederick Goldin, George Economou, Esther Quinn, and Saul Brody. To Carolyn Heilbrun, the dedication is but a slight acknowledgment of my gratefulness for the years of stimulating talk.

Chapter One

Biblical Exegesis

Of the various genres covered in this study, biblical exegesis is the least sympathetic to women, particularly in the centuries preceding the twelfth. The danger woman poses to man's moral state is introduced into Judaeo-Christian tradition with Eve's temptation of Adam and dominates the moral attitude towards women thenceforth. By her very nature, her physical beauty, woman has the power to seduce man from his purpose, to draw him down from his proper realm of thought to her realm of matter. Since it is the lower impulse in man that is susceptible to woman's attractions, that impulse—carnality, the desires of the flesh—is identified with women. Man is the *spiritus* (masc.), the higher rational soul, woman the *anima* (fem.), the lower sensible soul.[1] Every woman is Eve, the part of man that is vulnerable to the temptations of the devil, the part responsible for his fall from grace. And those women to whom the bible ascribes, instead, great moral strength—Judith, Esther, Ruth—are divested of their human nature by commentators and are made to represent impersonal abstractions like the church; even the bride of the Canticles is identified in early exegesis primarily with the collective church. The women in the New Testament who followed Christ and remained loyal when his disciples wavered are passed over quickly or explained away.

In the twelfth century, however, the philosophical and psychological concern for the individual moves exegesis in a different direc-

---

[1] "Possumus in viro spiritum, in muliere animam accipere" (*Glossa Ordinaria, Ecclus.* 25:2; *Patrologia Latina,* 113, 1211); cf. *Gl. Ord. Ep. ad Hebr.* 4:12; PL, 114, 650–51, "per animam intelliguntur carnalia peccata, id est quae actu corporis fiunt, ut luxuria. Per spiritum vero spiritualia, id est quae sunt mentis, ut superbia."

tion. In commentaries on the Canticles, the emphasis shifts to the human soul as the bride. In this marriage metaphor, man stands in relation to God as woman to man, so the writer must identify with the woman, the bride, in his relation to God, the bride-groom. Similarly, contemporary concern with the individual realizing his potential on earth, his desire to return to or at least strive for a pre-lapsarian harmony,[2] also encourages a different attitude towards women—a less critical view of the Eve who was created to share paradise with man, and of the nature and purpose of their relationship. It is significant that the allegory of the four daughters of God—Mercy, Justice, Truth, and Peace, four women who had been man's companions until he sinned and then debated his redemption before God—is also introduced into Christian culture in the early twelfth century.[3]

In the brief and necessarily superficial survey of biblical exegesis that follows, I have confined myself to interpretations of Genesis and the Song of Songs as the most fruitful material for this subject. For the attitudes of the early Middle Ages, I consulted a selection of the most influential commentators—Augustine, Gregory, Isidore, Rabanus Maurus, and the *Glossa Ordinaria* (a twelfth-century compilation of earlier exegetes). In the twelfth century, I concentrated on writers who were deeply involved in contemporary intellectual and cultural developments—Bernard of Clairvaux, Abelard, Hugh of St. Victor, Alanus de Insulis—who may be considered representative of, if not responsible for, major currents of twelfth-century thought, secular as well as religious.

One must be wary of suggesting any consistency of attitude in

---

[2] The desire to fulfill man's potential lies behind the substantial developments of educational curricula, e.g., Hugh of St. Victor's *Didascalion,* Thierry's *Heptateuchon;* the search for the ideal society is reflected in the Utopian background of much early romance.

[3] H. Traver, *The Four Daughters of God* (Philadelphia: J. C. Winston, 1907), p. 11. The allegory, based on verse 11 of the 84th Psalm, is introduced into Christian literature, probably from the Midrash, by Hugh of St. Victor in his *Annotationes in Psalmos;* Bernard of Clairvaux uses it in the First Sermon for the Annunciation of the Virgin Mary.

medieval exegesis, but, on the subject of women, there is a striking uniformity: bad women, like Delilah or Potiphar's wife, represent lower human characteristics, weaknesses of the flesh; good women stand for impersonal abstractions like the church. The connection of woman with the flesh, with matter, is at least partly based on her biological function, her ability to give birth. She is called "mother," Isidore explains, because from her something is effected; for mother is the matter, father the cause (*Etym.* IX, v, 5–6).[4] By the fact of her sex, then, woman is less inclined to things of the spirit. Her menstruation is also indicative of something unclean, figuratively as well as physically; it is said to signify bad thoughts, hence men who touch women while they are menstruating will defile their own thoughts. The physical state of menstruation denotes real moral corruption for the commentator; those who conceive children during this period bring forth deformed infants who expose their parents' sins for all to see (*Gl. Ord., Isa.* LXIV, 6; PL 113, 1308). For men, the corresponding physical feature which denotes a moral state is the foreskin which can, indeed must, be cut off. Circumcision represents the restraining of lust in the flesh, and it is the sign of salvation for mankind between Moses and Christ; only the circumcised are saved. This ability to cut off the physical symbol of his lust is so distinctly a male prerogative that some commentators feel obliged to explain that women can still be saved, even though they cannot be circumcised—but only in the old, pre-Law way, by faith. Hugh of St. Victor, in his work on the Sacraments, explains that circumcision is given only to males because sacred scripture is accustomed to signify the soul by a man, sex and flesh by a woman; so exterior circumcision conferred sanctification on souls but did not take away corruption from the flesh.[5] Abelard, in an untraditional comment, suggests that Christ consecrated female geni-

---

[4] Cf. *Gl. Ord. Ex.* 1:22; PL 113, 188: "Ubicumque in Scripturis femina legitur et sexus fragilior, ad materiae intelligentiam transferamus...feminas, quae materiae sunt vicinae...."

[5] *De sacramentis christianae fidei*, PL 176, 173–618. English translation, *Sacraments of the Christian Faith*, R. J. Deferrari (Cambridge: Medieval Academy of America, 1951).

tals more by his birth than male genitals by circumcision (*Ep.* 7),
though he adopts the figurative convention when he speaks of his own
castration: it *circumcised* me in mind as well as body and fitly in that
the member that committed the sin in enjoyment expiated it in pain
(*Ep.* 5).[6]

The act of intercourse, which involves the sinful impulse of
lust, is morally dangerous to man. This is why the eunuch, who is
disparaged in the Old Testament, is interpreted as a spiritual man in
medieval exegesis. It is why the most highly respected woman is the
virgin, next is the widow, and lowest in the hierarchy of good women
is the matron. The glory of the Virgin Mary was, of course, that she
could be the mother of a living son without carnal intercourse. Conception by the normal sexual process is the means by which original
sin is passed on, along with life: man is born, according to Gregory,
by the agency of woman, who was made subject to sin and passes on
to her children the frailty of the first guilt.[7]

Besides these purely biological facts, there are qualities of
character generally ascribed to women which lend themselves to similar interpretations: weakness and changeableness. Throughout the
Moralia, Gregory personifies the mind, which he connects with Job's
wife, as female because it is changeable, easily alarmed and agitated,
and open to surprise and deception (see particularly, I, 49 and 78).
The minds of men who serve God with yielding purpose are, he says,
not undeservedly called women (III, 40), whereas those who follow

[6] Latin edition of the letters by J. T. Muckle and T. P. McLaughlin in *Medieval Studies*
12 (1950), 163–213, 15 (1953), 47–94, 17 (1955), 240–81, and 18 (1956), 241–92.
There has been controversy over the authenticity of the letters. See E. Gilson, *Héloïse et
Abélard* (Paris: Lib. Phil. Vrin, 1964), Appendix I, which covers the arguments up to
that point; he admits that the attribution is not beyond question, but he accepts them, as
do R. W. Southern, *Medieval Humanism* (New York: Harper and Row, 1970), II, and
M. McLaughlin, "Abelard as Autobiographer: The Motives and Meaning of his *Story of
Calamities,*" *Speculum* 42 (1967), 463–88.

[7] *Moralium libri, sive expositio in librum Job (Moralia in Job)*, PL 75. English translation, *Morals on the Book of Job* by St. Gregory the Great, 3 vol., trans. by members of
the English church (Oxford: Parker, 1847).

the ways of the Lord with firm and steady steps are men (XXVIII, 12). The mind is the door-keeper of the soul; if it is female, that is, given to carnal thoughts, it allows evil to enter (III, 61). Thus Job's wife is the ladder by which the devil hopes to enter Job's fortress as he had Adam's through Eve (III, 12). Ironically, Wisdom is also personified as a woman in the *Moralia* (as in the Book of Wisdom), but she insists she can speak only to men, because those who are of unstable mind, women, cannot understand her (XXVIII, 12).[8]

Man is by nature thought to be strong, virile, constant, reasonable; whereas woman is inherently weak and prone to vice. When you see men who lead lives of voluptuousness, we are told in a commentary on Exodus, you know that in them the king of Egypt, the devil, kills the males and keeps the females alive (*Gl. Ord. Ex.* 1:15; PL 113, 186). That this is more than a figure of speech is clear from another passage in the same commentary: none of the holy men is said to have begotten females, or only rarely; Salphaat alone had all daughters and he died in sin (*Gl. Ord. Ex.* 1:22; PL 113, 188).

What happens in these interpretations is that the object of man's temptation becomes the cause of it; in other words, he projects his own weakness onto its object. His seduction may be either physical or intellectual. Whores are connected with heresy as well as with carnal lust; indeed, fornication and heresy (the allurement of superficial beauty, whether of body or word) are almost synonymous in much exegesis. The whore seduces with sweet words and with the beauty of her body as the heretic seduces with attractive doctrines (*Gl. Ord. Prov.* 5:3; PL 113, 1087). Here, too, an attempt is made to trace the effect to the nature of woman, to her tendency to lewd movement and the resultant flowing of her robes (*Gl. Ord. Deut.* 22:5; PL 113, 478). Once again, the connection is not merely figurative; there is literal basis for it in the stories of wise men, like Solomon, led into the worship of idols by their love for foreign women. And there is a psychological confusion as well, an implicit suggestion that the love of

---

[8] Her remark is a commentary on *Prov.* 8:4, "O viri, ad vos clamito."

woman is idolatrous, distracting man from the proper object of his worship. Alanus, in his *Distinctiones,* provides an interesting example of the way this sort of interpretation turns back on itself: women typify heresy, he says, flattering with warm persuasions; heretical doctrines are sweeter for they always teach enjoyment of the flesh, whereas the church orders abstention from carnal desires.[9] In other words, women represent heresy because heresy encourages hedonism and women are the objects of hedonism.

Generally, anti-feminist attitudes are so prevalent in the *Glossa* that the commentator feels obliged to explain, when a woman is singled out to perform a good action instead of a man, why that should be. This is particularly so in commentaries on the gospels, which emphasize the faith and constancy of Christ's followers. There are many women who attend him, some who even carry the word. They stay with him through his trials and never betray or deny him as Peter and Judas do. The commentators admit that the women loved more fiercely (*arctius amabant*) [10] but rarely do they accord these women a symbolic significance. However, they do offer explanations for the presence of women in the stories, usually to introduce a negative note where none exists, or to play down the defects of the men and the virtues of the women. Why should a girl recognise Peter at the gate, the commentator asks? Because, we are told, the ancient enemy seduced the first parent through a woman, so, through a woman he counsels the prince of the church to deny the teacher whom he had acknowledged as the son of God (*Gl. Ord. Mt.* 26:69; PL 114, 172). In the commentary on the same event as recounted by Luke, Peter is exonerated even further. We are told that he denies Christ not on the mountain, in the temple, or in the home, but in the palace of the Jews, where there is no truth. Peter would not have wandered in had it not been for a female porter. Thus, as Eve led Adam astray (*male induxit*) so the

---

[9] *Liber in Distinctiones Dictionum Theologicalium,* PL 120, 704; the remarks are made under the heading *aqua.*

[10] *Gl. Ord. Mt.* 27:61; PL 114, 177 and *Lk.* 23:55; 114, 350.

porter lets Peter in to lead him astray (*male introduxit*) (*Lk.* 22:57; PL 114, 342). Why, the commentator asks in another passage, are we told that the women wept at the cross? Not, he assures us, because only women wept, but because the female sex, as the more contemptible, could afford to show what it felt before the priests (*Lk.* 23:27; PL 114, 346). Why should a woman be the first to see the resurrected Christ? Because a woman was the author of man's guilt and death; so, lest she sustain the shame of perpetual guilt among men, she who had transferred her guilt to man now transfers grace. But, since the inferior sex does not have the constancy of preaching or the strength of execution, the office of evangelizing is transferred to men, to the apostles; the doubts of the apostles at the news she brings are voiced not because of their weakness but in order to strengthen us (*Mk.* 16:11; PL 114, 242–43; *Lk.* 24:11; PL 114, 351).

An even more curious twist is given to the story of the Samaritan woman at the well. In the Gospel, John 4, Christ tells her to call her husband in order to force her to admit that she has had five husbands and the man she now lives with cannot be called her husband. She recognizes that He is a prophet and the Messiah, and goes to carry the message into the city. The commentator interprets her as a figure for the church of the gentiles but goes on to say that when Christ told her to go call her husband, He meant that the sensual part of the soul should call on the rational intellect by which she is to be ruled as by a man (PL 114, 372)—as if Christ had told her to be subject to her husband when in fact He denied the validity of the marriage.

Abelard's comment on this story is strikingly different: we see, he tells us, in Christ's meeting with the Samaritan woman, how He longed for her salvation the more keenly, the more admirable He knew her virtue to be. Through her, He sought to quench His thirst for the salvation of women (*Ep.* 6). Abelard's comments on biblical events generally present an interesting contrast to the standard attitude expressed in the *Gloss*. This is not to say that he denies the conventional view altogether—there are passages in the letters and in the commentary on the Hexaemeron that might have been written by any of the commentators cited in the *Gloss*.[11] But Abelard turns the clichés of female weakness to women's advantage, emphasizing the greatness of their virtue when it asserts itself despite the weakness: as their sex is weaker, so their virtue is more pleasing to God and more perfect (*Ep*. 6). It is in his praise of their faith and devotion and the power of their prayers that Abelard differs from the exegetic tradition we have been discussing. He points out that the prayers of women can wipe out the sins of men, that such prayers can prevail over justice, and that nuns, as the wives of Christ, have greater power to move their husband by their prayers than other members of the household (*Ep*. 2). He points to virtuous women in the Bible and throughout Christian history: the wife of Clovis who led him to the faith when the preaching of saints could not (*Ep*. 2); women of the Old Testament who succeeded in great deeds where men had failed (*Ep*. 6); women who devoted themselves to the study of Christ and Christian philosophy, who were not separated from men in the things which pertained to God and religion (*Ep*. 6). He praises the faith of women like Elizabeth who recognized God while He was still in the womb, whereas her son, John, had to see Him to know Him as God. And he praises their devotion: they never deserted Christ; they stayed with Him at the cross. Indeed, he says, John speaks as if he had been called back by their example (*Ep*. 6). Christ singled out women by special signs again and again: the greatest miracles of resuscitation were displayed to women, were worked on women, or worked for them (*Ep*. 2); the Gospel records only women ministering to the Lord—He washed the feet of his disciples,

[11] E.g., the male is the rational soul, created in the image of God and taking his beginning from God, while the female is at one remove, only a similitude of God, taking her beginning from man (*Hexaemeron*, PL 178, 761); the weaker sex needs the stronger, hence man was appointed over woman as her head (*Hist. cal.*); women cause even wise men to go astray (*Ep*. 4); faithful women are distinguished from the women who desire earthly things and who as less perfect beings are rightly called daughters rather than sons (*Ep*. 4). Heloise expresses the same views more strongly, citing numerous examples of bad women to show how the devil uses women to destroy men just as he had used her (*Ep*. 3). For a detailed study of Abelard's views on women, see M. M. McLaughlin, "Peter Abélard and the Dignity of Women: Twelfth Century 'Feminism' in Theory and Practice," *Actes*, Colloque International P. Abélard—P. le Vénérable (in press).

but only women washed His, and Christ's head was anointed by women, his body by men (*Ep.* 6); women were chosen to see the risen
Christ first because they had watched sleepless at His sepulchre,
showing not by words but by deeds how much they loved Him
(*Ep.* 6). Christ showed that the female sex is essential to salvation
when He chose to assume His human body through a woman; he
could, Abelard suggests, have assumed it through a man, just as God
formed the first woman from the body of a man (*Ep.* 6). Even on the
creation of the first woman, Abelard departs from tradition: he notes
that she was created within Paradise, which is therefore her native
country, while man was created outside, and he points out that it is
outside, in an inferior place, that man is considered better than woman
(*Ep.* 6). In the Hexaemeron he says that woman was created in a better
place but became worse by her fall (PL 178, 776).

One is tempted to look for some relation between the unusually
positive view of biblical women Abelard expresses in his letters and
his own relations with Heloise. Whether or not one is prepared to go
as far as Gilson and posit Heloise's love for Abelard as Abelard's
model for the ideal love of man for God,[12] it is difficult to imagine
that her intellect and devotion did not have something to do with his
more sympathetic view of women. It is possible, of course, that
Abelard overemphasizes the dignity of women in order to strengthen
Heloise's spiritual resolve: "for you who bring forth spiritual progeny
for the Lord," he tells her, "it would be a great loss to bear children
for the world . . . you would not then be, as you are now, more than
a woman, transcending even men and turning the curse of Eve into the
blessing of Mary" (*Ep.* 4). It may be partly to excuse his own concern
for her and her nuns: he points to the examples of Jerome and Origen,
who also devoted time to the teaching of women, and notes that
Origen castrated himself in order to do so without scandal (*Hist. cal.*
and *Ep.* 6). Whatever his reasons, Abelard's comments on religious

[12] E. Gilson, *The Mystical Theology of St. Bernard* (New York: Sheed and Ward,
1940), Appendix II.

women are positive and unusual, perhaps more indicative of one ex-
ceptional mind than of a trend in the exegetic tradition, but occurring,
significantly, in the first half of the twelfth century.

The only biblical women, apart from the Virgin, who are
treated well by traditional commentators are those who are described
as shining examples of virtue—who cannot be made to represent
weakness or vice—and they are almost invariably said to symbolize
the church. Judith and Esther represent the church because they pun-
ished the enemies of the faith and saved God's people from destruction; Ruth is the church of the Gentiles, because she was a foreigner
who married a Jew and remained faithful to his people; Mary and
Martha, better known as figures for the active and contemplative life,
may also represent the church—Martha, the church in this life, doing
the work of justice, and Mary, the church in the future, resting in contemplation of divine wisdom.[13] But since the church is the congrega-
tion of men in all their weaknesses, reformed sinners as well as saints,
it can also be represented by women like Raab in the Old Testament
and Mary Magdalene in the New, both former prostitutes. Similarly,
the woman taken in adultery represents the church of the Gentiles,
which had "fornicated" by worshipping idols and which the zealous
Synagogue wished to destroy, but which Christ saved by the remission
of sins.

The most important instance of the church identified with a
woman is, of course, that of the bride in the Canticles. It is in this love
affair between God and His church that we find the strongest antidote
to the anti-feminism of theologians, since it forces the male writer and
his audience to identify with the female role. Here the bride is not
merely the lower sensible part of the soul; instead she represents the
whole man or mankind in the assembly of the faithful, which must rise
or fall by her devotion. The marriage of Christ and the church, a figure deriving from Christ's own reference to himself as the bridegroom,
is a topos in the vocabulary of medieval exegesis. It occurs regularly

[13] Isidore, *Allegoriae Quaedam Sacrae Scripturae,* PL 83, 124–25.

in passages having nothing to do with the Canticles, e.g., heretics and schismatics commit the worst form of incest, for they corrupt by error the church, the bride of Christ (*Gl. Ord. Deut.* 27:20; PL 113, 483). The popularity of this metaphor extends even to religious drama, as in the twelfth-century plays about the Wise and Foolish Virgins. It is such a generally accepted figure that even the physical beauty of a woman can be good in this connection:

> Assimilaverit eam mulieri pro perfectione, pro speciositate, pro singulorum dispositione graduum, pro decentis unitatis compositione.
>
> [*Gl. Ord. Cant.* 4:12; PL 113, 1150]
>
> He compared her to a woman for her perfection, her beauty, the disposition of individual parts, the composition of fitting unity.

Most commentators on the Canticles say the bride may be either the church or the human soul, but early commentators concentrate their remarks on the church. In Origen, the spiritual love of Christ and the church is contrasted with physical love, and the love of wisdom with the love of women.[14] Origen admits that love is a natural emotion of the soul (Hom. II, i), and that the love for women—mothers, sisters, even wives—can be pure (Hom. III, 7), but the proper object of our love is wisdom and truth (Hom. II, 1). Woman is imperfect, hence not the safest object for love. Even the bride (who as the church is the assembly of saints) is imperfect, since she is also a woman: Christ gathered the church from the prostitution of many philosophic doctrines and put the necklace of obedience on her neck (Hom. II, 7), but she does not keep her vineyard (II, 3). It is not surprising, Origen comments, that the bride should be guilty of such faults, when we remember how the first woman was seduced.

Bernard's Sermons on the Song of Songs, written in the twelfth century, focus more on the love between Christ and the individual soul, which is consummated in marriage because marriage represents the highest form of human love:

---

[14] *Commentary and Homilies on the Song of Songs,* trans. R. P. Lawson (Westminster: Newman Press, 1957).

> Love is the highest of natural gifts . . . the affection between the
> word, Christ, and the soul cannot be more sweetly expressed than by
> calling them bridegroom and bride. . . . All is held in common
> between them . . . they are one flesh (VII, ii, 2).[15]
> Theirs is a truly spiritual contract, more than a contract, an embrace,
> which makes one spirit of two (LXXXIII, i, 3). . . .
> The bride's love is the highest degree of human love; the groom
> requires nothing else, she has nothing else to give, that is why they are
> called bride and groom. This kind of love is unique to married people
> . . . no one else attains it, not even a child and parent (LXXXIII,
> i, 5).
> No one can understand the canticles unless he loves (LXXIX, i). . . .
> but if he loves perfectly, he can dare to aspire to marriage with the
> word (LXXXIII, i, 1).

Although Bernard speaks here and elsewhere of a love that strongly
suggests the physical union of male and female, even at times with
sexual overtones,[16] and although he acknowledges our need for the
body in order to prepare our spirits to reach salvation (V, i. 1), the
love he intends us to understand is purely spiritual. Despite his remarks about marriage and his use of sensual imagery, Bernard has no
feeling for the love between man and woman. His sermons are written
for men, even more narrowly for those men already vowed to a religious life, and his views on women, whether dictated by his audience
or by personal preference, do not differ markedly from those of the
Gloss. When the bride is called beautiful among women, Bernard
says, women signify carnal and secular souls, which have nothing
virile in them, which show nothing strong or constant in their acts,
which are completely languid, soft, feminine (XXXVIII, iii, 4). But
Bernard's devotion to the Virgin knows no bounds. Although he

[15] *Sermones in Cantica Canticorum,* ed. LeClerq, Talbot, Rochais, (Rome: Editiones
Cisterciences, 1957), 2 vol.

[16] E.g., the arrow which pierces the soul of Mary, leaving no part of her virgin breast
empty of love (XXIX, iv, 8); the angel as *paranymphus,* the go-between that encourages
the soul's love for God, even bearing gifts and arranging meetings between them
(XXXI, ii, 5).

makes relatively little of the Virgin as Christ's beloved in his comments on the Canticles, he glorifies her in other sermons as the mother
of God. She is unique, not only among women but in comparison to
all mankind:

> Despite the infinite difference between the flesh which the son obtains
> from his mother and the divinity from his father, he is one, wholly and
> entirely the son of both (Fourth Sermon on the Glories of the Virgin).
> It was by means of her faith that the word was united to flesh (Second
> Sermon for Christmas).
> She is represented as clothed with the sun because she has penetrated
> the unfathomable abyss of divine wisdom to an almost incredible de-
> gree . . . she is as completely immersed in that ocean of inaccessible
> light as is possible to any created nature. . . . Mary has merited far
> more than the prophets or the Seraphim (Sermon for Sunday within
> Octave of Assumption).[17]

She is an active force, through her faith and purity, in the incarnation
of God and, therefore, in the salvation of man.

Bernard's devotion to the Virgin is such that he can identify
himself, through her, with a woman's role, and speak of himself as a
mother to his monks.[18] But it is Alanus de Insulis (whose allegories
will be discussed in Chapter Two), who consistently interprets the
bride of the Canticles as the Virgin:

> The Virgin, desiring the presence of her spouse, says let him kiss me
> with the kiss of his mouth, that is, the word of God, Christ, through
> which the father speaks to the world. . . .
> She is properly mother as well as beloved for her breasts nourish the
> faithful with the two exemplars of good living, chastity and humility

---

[17] St. Bernard's *Sermons for the Seasons and the Principal Festivals of the Year*, trans.
by a priest of Mt. Melleray, 3 vol., (Westminster: The Carroll Press, 1950). Latin edition *Sermones de tempore, de sanctis, de diversis* (Wien, 1891).

[18] E.g., "when a mother gives birth, she suffers, but I would forget the pain, holding
the fruit of it, which Christ has formed in my offspring" (*Sermones in Cant.*, XXIX,
iii, 6); "for what mother, even though she knows she has done all she can for her ailing
son, and when she sees it was in vain and he is dying, can refrain her tears? So it is no
consolation to me if I see my son die, that I have done my duty by him" (XLII, iii).

> . . . her breasts are two arms of charity, one loves Christ as God, the
> other as son.
>
> [*Elucidatio in Cantica Canticorum,* I] [19]

It is, of course, particularly fitting to see the bride of the Canticles as a
prefiguration of the Virgin, since she, of all mankind, loved God so
perfectly that she was able to bear fruit, physically as well as spiritually, body and soul, achieving in this life the full use of the two inseparable parts of human nature, and doing so without sin. She is, in
this sense, the most perfect human being of those born of human
parents. To cast the Virgin, a historical woman, in the woman's role
in this love song, not just by an occasional reference but by a consistent interpretation, is unusual and significant. It forces both writer and
reader to go a step beyond the normal process in which the man's soul
is identified with a woman's role in its love for God; here he must not
simply identify with a fictional woman who, it is universally held, represents man, but with a real woman, who lived the role literally as
well as figuratively.

We have, then, two opposing traditions in scriptural exegesis—
woman as the source and symbol of man's fall, and woman as the
source and symbol of his salvation. In giving birth to Christ, the
Virgin Mary is the immediate source of salvation, thereby exonerating
Eve and all her daughters; it is said also of the women surrounding
Christ that their acts are meant to make up for the woman whose trans-
gression made Christ's coming necessary. In some ways, both views
of woman converge on Eve: Eve was the first woman to fall, but she is
also the first to be led out of Hell by Christ; she was guilty of original
sin but she is also a symbol of the church; she succumbed to the devil
but she is the mother of the human race. All other women are, in some
way, Eve, so it is in analyses of her position and function that we may
expect to find the most complicated and, for secular literature, probably the most pertinent attitudes towards woman. The questions most

[19] PL 120, 51–110.

frequently asked are: why did God create a female rather than a male companion for Adam, and what was the nature of their relations? Though their union has allegorical significance both figuratively and morally (it prefigures the union of Christ and the church and it symbolizes the wedding of the lower and higher soul in Man, or the flesh and spirit), at the same time it is, and must be taken as, a real marriage between a man and a woman. As such, its nature must be understood as it was meant to be (before sin) and as it became (after the fall)—what it is ideally, and what it must be for fallen man.[20]

For this study, Hugh of St. Victor's comments are the most interesting. Some of what he says is traditional—much had been said by Augustine—but there are important differences. There is no disagreement about the first question, why Adam was given a female companion; the answer is always, of course, for progeny. Before the fall, offspring would have been produced without sin (Hugh, Sac. I, vi, 23); cf. Augustine, the organs of generation would have served without lust as the hands and feet do, indeed the male semen would have entered the woman's womb without destroying her virginity, as the menses come out (Civ. Dei, XIV, 23 and 26).[21] Hugh emphasizes the importance of both parties in procreation (what is possible for neither alone is possible for each through the other), and the need for love, and mutual esteem, which alone can extort this debt from nature (Sac. II, i, 8). For both Hugh and Augustine, there is more to marriage than procreation; the natural companionship between the sexes is an essen-

[20] For a study of medieval theological views on the marriage in Eden, see Michael Müller, *Die Lehre des Heiligen Augustinus von der Paradiesehe und ihre Auswirkung in der Sexualethik des 12 und 13 Jahrhunderts bis Thomas von Aquin,* Studien zur Geschichte der Katholischen Moraltheologie, I, (Regensburg: Friedrich Pustet, 1954).

[21] At times Augustine seems to intend a spiritual fetus of "intelligible and immortal joys" (*De Genesi contra Manichaeos,* I, xix, Sancti Aurelii Augustini *Opera omnia,* post Lovaniensium Theologorum Recensionem, opera et studio Monachorum Ordinis Sancti Benedicti, Vol. 3, Pt. 1), resulting from a spiritual copulation; but at other times he says that sons born by the affection of pious charity alone would fill the earth with just and holy people (*De Genesi ad Litteram,* III, xxi; *Opera omnia,* 3, 1).

tial part of it (Augustine, *De bono coniugali*,[22] Hugh, Sac. II, xi, 3). In a good marriage, Augustine says, after the ardor of youth cools charity still flourishes; the relation improves as the sexual element, by mutual consent, disappears (*De b. con.*, ibid.). Even after the fall, marriage did not become an evil because of incontinence; instead, incontinence is venial in relation to the good of marriage (*De Gen. ad Litt.* IX, vii). For Hugh, the essence of marriage is the pure love of mind, the mutual consent of loving spirits. Eve, he says, was formed from Adam's side to show that she was created for love, not as mistress or handmaid; not from the head, to dominate, or from the feet, to be his slave; she was to be his companion, to be placed beside him, for equality of association (Sac. I, vi, 35). She was also made from him so that she might always look to him as to her beginning, just as all men, coming from one, should be one and love one another as if they were one (Sac. I, vi, 34).[23] In other words, marriage is the basic unit of human relations around which all society is built. It is the one sacrament, according to Hugh, which was instituted before the fall (Sac. I, viii, 13).

We have seen why there must be male and female in human and social terms. Now let us consider the symbolic importance of the two sexes. We are told in Genesis that God created man in His image and also that He created male and female. Augustine interprets man in the first instance (*homo*) to stand for the human species. In this sense, both male and female are ''man'' (''secundum id quod et femina homo erat,'' *De Gen. ad Litt.* III, xxii), equal in mind and reason inasmuch as both are made in the image of God. However, Augustine adds, lest we think that only the spirit of man was created, the Bible makes the further distinction between male and female to make it clear

---

[22] St. Augustine, *Treatises on Marriage and Other Subjects,* trans. C. T. Wilcox, in *The Fathers of the Church,* Vol. 27 (New York: Fathers of the Church, 1955), p. 12.

[23] Cf. Augustine, *Civ. Dei,* XII, 21 and *De b. con.,* p. 9. Human nature is social, Augustine points out; it possesses the capacity for friendship. God therefore created all men from one so that they would be held together in society not just by similarity but by blood relation.

that he was created in body as well as in spirit. In other words, the perfection of the human species lies in the existence of both male and female, both soul and body. Once the difference is established, however, a hierarchy is inevitable. Just as Christ is the head of His church, so man is the head of woman. The creation of Eve from the sleeping Adam's side foreshadows and signifies the creation of the church from the side of the dying Christ. The woman represents, then, a lower part of man: she may be either the body, the animal part, the flesh, which should be one in desire with the spirit (*De Gen. c. Man.* II, xii), or she may be the appetite of soul, which should be subject to virile reason (ibid., II, xi). It was cupidity (Eve), led by the serpent, that induced the reason (Adam) to sin. For Hugh, also, Eve represents a lower part of the soul, but he raises her from the symbol of sensibility and concupiscence, which in his scheme is represented by the serpent, to the rational soul, prudence; prudence is meant to dominate sensibility but be subject to higher reason (Adam), which directs its attention to the divine and invisible (Sac. I, viii, 13).

It is here that Hugh differs markedly from earlier interpreters. But because he attributes a higher symbolic position to Eve, he also holds her more responsible for what happens. Augustine had said that Adam shared responsibility for the fall inasmuch as it was reason's duty to hold cupidity back; he chose to join Eve, although he himself would not have been deceived by the devil, either because he believed she would waste away without him (*De Gen. ad Litt.* XI, xlii) or because he could not bear to be separated from his only companion (*Civ. Dei* XIV, 11).[24] Augustine allows Adam both a selfish and a compassionate motivation, but in either case the devil would not have been able to trap him had man not already begun to live for himself (*Civ. Dei* XIV, 13), so he bears a good part of the responsibility. Bernard blames Adam for attempting to shift the guilt onto his wife (Sermon for Feast of All Saints): in sinning for Eve's sake, Adam was

[24] It is tempting to see an autobiographical element in this explanation. Augustine admits to the same problem in the *Confessions,* saying that for pleasure and comfort he cannot live without a woman; however, he never blames women for leading him astray.

criminally compassionate when he should have been kindly cruel, but in not accepting the responsibility for Eve's sake, he was criminally cruel when he should have been kindly compassionate. He should have said the woman is weak, she has been seduced, the sin is mine, let vengeance fall on me. But Hugh, although he also blames Adam for consenting to the sin and not correcting the sinner, holds Eve more guilty for having sinned out of voluntary wickedness, first pride and avarice, then sheer delight (Sac. I, vii, 8). She encouraged the devil by her doubts—he would not have dared approach her to deny the word of God had he not found doubt in her (Sac. I, vii, 4). She is responsible because she could have acted differently; she had the power to control her impulse, Hugh insists, attributing to her moral strength not usually conceded to women by theologians. Her instincts are not of themselves bad: Hugh shows that the same impulse that led to sin—delight—can work for good. Sometimes the just mind, in its own imperfection, is moved to serve God; it is attracted at first by some reward which is offered, and then, as it grows in love of goodness, it is held in His service by voluntary delight alone (Sac. I, vii, 8). The union of Adam and Eve represents for Hugh the betrothal of God to the rational spirit; marriage between the male and female is the sacrament and image of the relation of God to the soul (Sac. II, xi, 3). Man was to engender, woman to conceive and bear, so that in this similitude it might be shown that the rational soul could not bear fruit unless it first received the seed of virtue from God (Sac. I, viii, 13). Here, as in the interpretations of the Canticles, man represents God and woman represents man; the love between man and woman is not an obstacle to, but a figure for, the love between God and the soul.

Perhaps the most important point made about Eve in these commentaries is that she was created out of Adam because she was meant to be a part of him. They are not two, but one; only together do they represent the human species. Biologically, this may seem obvious, but psychologically it is an important principle. Eve represents a part of Adam which he must learn to control and use properly, not to reject, if he is to achieve the reintegration of the human being, and he must accomplish that before he can achieve union with God, the re-union with his creator which is his ultimate goal. From this point of view, woman has a positive role to play in the moral development of man, a role given her by God; [25] the responsibility is man's to see that she plays it. To blame her for leading him astray, to make her the scapegoat for his failure, is to abdicate his own role. This is clearly the easier path to take, and it is followed often enough in the material we have looked at and again in the thirteenth century (see Chapter Four). But the positive attitude towards woman, the identification with the bride, the acceptance of Eve as a part, not necessarily bad, of oneself, is reflected in much of the secular literature of the twelfth century and achieves its fullest expression in Dante's *Comedy* in the fourteenth.

[25] Cf. Hildegard of Bingen, *Causae et Curae*.

Chapter Two

Allegory[1]

In biblical exegesis, there are relatively few personified abstractions; little is done with Wisdom, the most striking of the Old Testament personifications, and the Four Daughters of God come into Christian writings only in the twelfth century. But the classical tradition is another matter. In Rome abstractions were personified and even worshipped as divinities; virtues were portrayed as women in classical art, a practice that continues in medieval art, even though the human, biblical, figures associated with the virtues were almost always men.[2] Many of the classical personifications were female because the abstract nouns they represent are feminine, though grammatical accident is not the only factor in determining gender. With concepts which have masculine as well as feminine names (e.g. *anima* and *animus*),[3] the choice may be determined by the qualities attributed to them. In any

[1] I am indebted to the American Council of Learned Societies for a grant which enabled me to do most of the research for this chapter and for the Appendix.

[2] On the virtues in classical murals and mosaics, see M. W. Bloomfield, *The Seven Deadly Sins*, p. 33; on the female personifications and male exempla, with the exception of Judith, see A. Katzenellenbogen, *Allegories of the Virtues and Vices in Medieval Art*, Pt. II, Ch. i–ii. There was also a strong tradition in Greek and Roman religions of the mother goddess—life-giving, loving, and at times devouring [Erich Neumann, *The Origins and History of Consciousness*, trans. R. F. C. Hull, Bollingen Series, 42 (Princeton University Press, 1954).]

[3] This is a complicated problem. Originally, *animus* was connected with the spiritual or intellectual principle as opposed to the physical, while *anima* meant simply the vital force, the breath of life. This is still so in Isidore: "anima vitae est, animus consilii" (*Etym.* XI, i, 11). In Christian writing, though *animus* still means "mind," *anima* comes to mean the soul as opposed to the body, and in the case of the *anima mundi*,

case, there is a legacy from pagan culture of women representing virtues and good qualities which is brought into Christian tradition
through allegory and art.

There is, of course, an essential difference between an exegetic
and an allegorical tradition. In the former, we have established texts
and stories from which a meaning must be derived; in the latter, we
have a meaning for which a fable must be constructed. In exegesis, a
deeper meaning is found for history; in allegory, a higher reality is
translated into perceptible images. This does not mean that personifications were not taken seriously. On the contrary, abstract concepts were real forces. The early Christian writers spoke of moral
problems in terms of inner conflict, a mode they inherited from the
Romans (Seneca, Statius); they make them sound like real struggles.
Bloomfield tells us that the desert fathers considered sin an objective
power and believed that, in the form of demons, it could enter the
bodies of animals.[4] Hermetic and early monastic writers also conceived of sins as demons. The Gnostics believed that souls picked up
their sins as they passed through the planets on their way down to
earth and surrendered them again to the proper aerial demons when
they died. This belief seems to be echoed in the twelfth-century allegories of Bernard Silvester and Alanus de Insulis, in the care that is
taken to protect the soul against the influence of the spheres on its
journey from heaven to its body on earth. Both Alanus and Bernard
discuss the demonic influence on man (Bernard in the *De mundi universitate,* II, 7, and Alanus in the *Summa Quoniam Homines,* Bk. II,
Tract i, 146–49)[5] as does Guillaume de Conches in the *Dragmaticon*

---

originally the life-force in the world, it came to be identified by some as a separate entity, a world-soul, even confused with the Holy Spirit (see above, p. 5).

[4] The points taken from Bloomfield in this and the following sentence are discussed
in the first part of *The Seven Deadly Sins.* See particularly pp. 27, 47 ff, 61, and
79.

[5] The Latin text of the *De mundi universitate, libri duo sive Megacosmus et Microcos-
mus* was edited by C. S. Barach and J. Wrobel (1876; repr. Frankfurt: Minerva, 1964).
An English translation by W. Wetherbee has just appeared in the Columbia Records of

(Bk. I). Bernard's spirits, a lower class of angels who report the needs
of man to God, live along the lunar boundary; there is one "genius" to
watch over each man. Below the midpoint of air, there are evil spirits,
agents of the devil who inflict injury on men and "insinuate themselves
invisibly into minds that are at rest or concerned with their own
thoughts, through the power of suggestion" (II, 7). Alanus says something similar in the *Summa:* for each man, there is one good angel,
"ad custodiam," and one bad, "ad exercitium" (146); each bad angel
or demon tempts to one particular vice. Guillaume speaks of "rational
animals" of the air; the good one reports man's prayers to God, the
bad, envious of man's good, tries to incite him to dishonorable action.
The good demons he calls "kalodaimones," the bad, "kakodai-
mones." Fletcher's observation that a man possessed by a demon is
well on his way to being a personification of the demon's quality
points up the relation between the concept of demons and allegory.[6]

Whether sin and virtue indicate a higher force in possession of
a man or simply a supernatural influence, there is no question that
vices and virtues have a real existence for medieval men and the figures that personify these concepts in literature have more than a meta-
phoric relation to them. This is true not only of moral qualities, but of
all abstract concepts. In Barfield's words, "for the man of the Middle
Ages, Grammar or Rhetoric, Mercy or Daunger were real to begin
with, simply *because* they were 'names.' " [7] A belief in the ex-
tramental reality of universal concepts persists through the Middle
Ages, though it was emphasized more in the early Middle Ages, and
vigorously debated and somewhat modified in the course of the twelfth

Civilization Series (New York: Columbia, 1973), under the title *The Cosmographia of
Bernardus Silvestris*. The quotations in English are from this translation. Brian Stock,
Myth and Science in the Twelfth Century (Princeton, 1972) also refers to Bernard's
poem as *Cosmographia*. I have retained the title used by the editors of the Latin edition
for the reader's convenience. Alanus' *Summa Quoniam Homines* was edited by P.
Glorieux in *AHDL*, 20 (1954), 113–364.

[6] A. Fletcher, *Allegory, the Theory of a Symbolic Mode*, p. 48 ff.

[7] Quoted by M. W. Bloomfield in "A Grammatical Approach to Personification Allegory," *MPh*, 60 (1963), 170.

century. The Chartrians,[8] who are responsible for the major twelfth-century allegories that will be discussed in this chapter, tended towards realism, with some qualifications. Their Neo-Platonism involves them necessarily in the reality of metaphor: visible reality reflects invisible reality, the whole universe being a hierarchy with each level reflecting the one above it. Thus the symbol contains, in part, the essence of what it symbolizes. Allegory is a natural mode of expression for this kind of thought, offering a step beyond the visible universe towards the realm of forms.

The Chartrians turned to allegory particularly to deal with an important question in contemporary Neo-Platonism, the creation of this world and the relation of Plato's *Timaeus* to the teachings of Genesis.[9] For our purposes, the most interesting creation image in the *Timaeus* is sexual: as the mother receives the seed, so *ile* (*hyle*), matter, receives figures from the archetype; as offspring proceeds from father and mother, so the world proceeds from *ile* and the *archetypus mundi*. Matter is the mother who receives the species; providence, the sphere of divine ideas, is the father who supplies the image. Guillaume, in his commentary on the *Timaeus*,[10] interprets the union of Saturn and Rhea as an allegory of creation: Saturn is time, Rhea primordial matter or *ile;* their children, Jupiter and Juno, are fire and

[8] I continue to use the term "Chartrians" despite Southern's attack in "Humanism and the School of Chartres," *Medieval Humanism* (New York: Harper, 1970), pp. 61–85, because it is a useful means of identifying writers whose careers may not have been centered on Chartres, but who were there at some point, who influenced each other, and whose work has much in common, not the least of which are Neo-Platonism, the interest in creation and in science. Recent books on the work of Bernard and Alanus also continue to use the term [see G. Economou, *The Goddess Natura in Medieval Literature* (Cambridge: Harvard University, 1972), W. Wetherbee, *Platonism and Poetry in the Twelfth Century,* The Literary Influence of the School of Chartres (Princeton, 1972), and B. Stock, *Myth and Science.*]

[9] Bernard and Alanus wrote allegorical poems about it; Guillaume de Conches, Thierry, Clarembald of Arras, and Gilbert de Poitiers discussed it in philosophical tracts. See also J. M. Parent, *La Doctrine de la Création dans l'Ecole de Chartres* (Paris, Ottawa, 1938).

[10] Ed. E. Jeauneau, *Glossae super Platonem* (Paris: Vrin, 1965).

air, temporal and material. The father, the *archetypus mundi,* is the sum of the ideas that have been in the divine mind from eternity; he is divine wisdom, analogous to the second person of the trinity. Christ, the Word, the manifestation of God in time. The union of God's ideas with matter is spoken of, figuratively, as a sexual act.[11] Matter is the mother, the prime locus of all generation, the receptacle of all forms, which in itself forms nothing, i.e., the passive female, the womb which must receive the male seed (in this case divine ideas) before it can conceive. It may well be that such a metaphorical use of the sexual act as a figure of God's creation, exalts the human sexual act, enabling Bernard Silvester and Alanus to justify sex in their poetry as an essential tool in the work of providence. And if creation can be described as a sexual act, it is not surprising that creating forces analogous to the trinity are personified as female figures, as we will see in Bernard.[12]

All aspects of the created universe are spoken of in the Neo-Platonic tradition in terms of male and female—numbers (masculine if they are odd, feminine if even; Macrobius), music (rhythm masculine, melody feminine; Martianus).[13] Creation itself is the wedding of opposites, of matter and idea, body and soul. Marriage is thus an important figure in this, as in the Song of Songs tradition.[14] Man appreciates the harmony that results from the union of opposites and attempts to

[11] See Thierry, Commentary on *De Trinitate* of Boethius, ed. N. M. Haring, *AHDL,* 23 (1956), 257–325; Clarembald's *Tractatus super Librum Boetii de Trinitate,* ed. N. M. Haring in *Life and Works of Clarembald of Arras* (Toronto: Pontifical Institute, 1965); and Gilbert's commentary on the *De Trinitate,* ed. N. M. Haring, *The Commentaries on Boethius* (Toronto: Pontifical Institute, 1966).

[12] Once the world has been created, the Neo-Platonists speak of it as a body, vivified by the world soul, the *anima mundi,* the force which gives life to the universe, which was identified by some with the Holy Spirit (see above, p. 37, n. 3).

[13] One of the loveliest variations on this theme is to be found in St. Francis' *Laudes Creaturarum,* who praises God for "frate Sole" and "sora Luna," "frate Vento" and "sor'Aqua."

[14] Wetherbee makes a connection between the Song of Songs and Alanus' *De planctu,* p. 189. The marriage image is particularly striking in Martianus' *De nuptiis,* the commentaries on it, and the works that derived from it.

imitate it in his own activity, in the arts, creating order from diversity, and in his private life, creating a new man through union with his opposite, woman. At the same time, he strives to make his way back from the visible universe to its cause, for which he uses all the arts and sciences at his command. Synthesis is both the method and result of this process, synthesis of Plato and Aristotle, of philosophy or natural science and theology. Poetic intuition is the only means of linking philosophy and theology, Wetherbee suggests,[15] hence Bernard and Alanus express their ideas of creation and the relation of man and God in poetry. In fiction they can describe the workings of the trinity but avoid the philosophical difficulties encountered by Gilbert de Poitiers and Guillaume de Conches, and they can express insights into the nature of God by figures which discursive prose would not permit.[16] They can, for instance, show God to be both male and female, the ultimate union of opposites: Noys (or Nous), who represents the second person of the trinity, or an aspect thereof, is female, not only because the noun is feminine in Greek (Logos might have been used instead), but because creation begins with a kind of sexual act between God and Noys (see below, p. 56).

I am not suggesting that the personifications in the allegories under discussion are female because of an inherent femaleness in the concepts they embody, but rather that, because they are female and because there are various impulses to encourage the identification of the symbol with the thing symbolized, their female attributes are emphasized and their female powers exalted. And, in some instances, concepts normally expressed as masculine are represented by female figures. In allegory, then, women can be forces for good as well as evil; they can protect and nourish, not just seduce and destroy. Com-

[15] Wetherbee, p. 4.

[16] In philosophic tracts, one is more restricted by language: God must be masculine, according to Clarembald. He is referred to as father, not mother, as son, not daughter, because God is the most worthy of all things and the masculine sex is worthier than the feminine, because odd numbers are masculine, and because the male acts and does not suffer, the female suffers but does not act (Comm. on Boethius, *De Trinitate*, 20, 21).

menting on the figure of Philosophy in Boethius' *Consolation,* Guillaume de Conches tells us that she appears as a woman (*sub specie mulieris*) because she softens the ferocities of souls, nourishes children with her milk . . . because philosophy is feminine in Greek, or because women are better accustomed to tend the sick than men.[17] Medieval personification is just this combination of rhetorical necessity and psychological or physiological reality.

We will see that, in the moral allegories, women represent good, as well as evil, opposing forces that can pull man in either direction: the virtues and vices in Prudentius' *Psychomachia,* Philosophy and Fortune in Boethius' *Consolation.* Even in poems which have much broader scope, which I will call philosophical allegories, one finds a similar opposition: between Venus and Pallas-Minerva in Martianus' *De nuptiis;* between Nature and Venus in Alanus' *De planctu;* between Nature and Alecto, and the virtues and vices, in the *Anticlaudian.* But in these works, as in Bernard's *De mundi,* the most important role of woman is as the life-giver, the protector of God's plan. Marriage, as a metaphor for the reconciliation of opposites, as well as the means by which God's plan is carried out within the moral order, is a recurrent motif in most of the poems. I will limit my discussion to the works mentioned above, which are the most important allegories through the twelfth century. I have included the *Consolation* because of the importance of the personification of Philosophy in the allegorical tradition, although the work itself is not properly an allegory.

Prudentius is concerned in the *Psychomachia* with the overcoming of vices by virtues within the soul, the preparation of the soul for Wisdom's entrance. He begins the poem with a prologue which sets the example for man's action and reveals the goal to be achieved. It is a brief narration of certain episodes in the story of Abraham, Sarah, and Lot: Abraham's rescue of Lot from the enemy kings, the visit of the angels, and Sarah's conception. Prudentius tells us that we

[17] Manuscript, Paris, Bibl. nat., lat. 14380; Troyes, Bibl. mun. 1381, 36 v.

can "beget no child of wedlock pleasing to God whose mother is Virtue, till the spirit, battling valorously, has overcome . . . the monsters in the enslaved heart" (ll. 11–14).[18] Abraham is clearly the spirit (*spiritus*) here, Sarah is Virtue, and the enslaved heart is Lot. Abraham must free his heart, Lot, before his union with Sarah can be fruitful. In this case, Abraham and Lot together represent man—Abraham the spirit, Lot the body. The woman, Sarah, represents the good that is joined with the spirit, a significant difference from the exegetic traditions discussed in Chapter One, where woman usually represents the body or carnal desires. In standard commentaries, Lot is the just man threatened by the machinations of the wicked (see Gregory, *Moralia,* I, 1), the holy man freed from the fires of the impious at the end of the world (Isidore, *Allegoriae*), or Christ's body, which suffers at the hands of the impious but is freed (*Gl. Ord. Gen.* 19:15; PL 113, 131). He never represents the body or heart "enslaved to foul desires" as in Prudentius' poem. Sarah normally symbolizes the church or the New Testament (according to Isidore, Augustine in *Civ. Dei,* and Rabanus Maurus), not the soul and certainly not virtue; Gregory even interprets her as *cura carnis,* care for the flesh, as opposed to Abraham, *spiritualis intellectus,* when he goes to meet the angels and she remains behind.

        As Prudentius continues the story, he shifts the figural significance of the characters slightly. Once Abraham has freed Lot from base desires, Christ can enter the heart, enabling it to entertain the trinity (the three angels) and "the Spirit, embracing in holy marriage the soul that has long been childless, will make her fertile by the seed eternal" (ll. 64–66). Here Sarah is the soul (*animam*), in the sense that she conceives, and she is Abraham's soul; Abraham becomes Christ, whose presence in his heart enables him to beget the child. In other words, Abraham becomes God and Sarah is man, man standing in relation to God as woman does to man, as in interpretations of the

[18] *Prudentius* with an English trans. by H. J. Thomson, Loeb Classical Library (1949; repr. Cambridge: Harvard University, 1962).

Canticles. Their union and its fruit is man's goal—the presence of Wisdom, of Christ, in the individual mind, which man can achieve by overcoming the evil in his heart.

The bulk of the poem describes the struggle between good and evil within the soul, the forces of light and darkness, as the poet calls them at the end of the work (1. 908). Man is not of a simple nature (*non simplex natura hominis*, 904), but a double substance (*duplex substantia*, 909); the forces of good and evil, virtue and vice, are constantly at war within him. These forces are personified as women in the poem, but Prudentius does rather interesting things with the sexual identification. The virtues, as we might expect, are mannish, virile and strong, described as valiant warriors—with the exceptions of Patience (*Patientia*), who modestly waits for Wrath (*Ira Tumens*) to perish by her own hand, and Humility or Humble Mind (*Mens Humilis*), who must be encouraged by Hope (*Spes*) before she can cut off Pride's (*Superbia*) head. The vices, however, see the virtues quite differently: Pride accuses her enemies of being effeminate and soft; she complains that they are not stirred by the Goddess of War, that she and her fellows are disgraced by having to fight with "virgin choruses" (1. 242), their strength shamed by such a fragile triumph (*fragilique viros foedare triumpho*, 1. 252). Ironically, it is the deception of her ally, Fraud (*Fraus*), acting more like a treacherous woman than a valiant warrior, which undoes her: Fraud prepares a trap into which Pride falls. The irony is increased by the reaction of the now victorious opponent, Humility, who hesitates to cut off the dead Pride's head, a weakness that would have elicited the latter's contempt.

Prudentius is clearly using the reverse of expectation, in this case a confusion of sexual roles, to make a moral point about the relative strength and weakness of vices and virtues. Having shown the fierce Pride and Anger to be more vulnerable than we expected, and the gentle Humility and Patience to be more forceful, he shifts again in later encounters, and shows effeminate vices to be unexpectedly successful. Indulgence (*Luxuria*), who appears with perfumed hair, shifty glances, and languid voice, her life given over to pleasure, captures the hearts of her enemies by throwing violets and roses from her chariot instead of weapons. The virtues throw down their arms to become her slaves, covering their virile heads with gilt turbans, exchanging their armor for ointments and long gowns (352) ff), until Soberness (*Sobrietas*) rallies them with the cross. Avarice runs around the battlefield, not fighting, but picking up whatever she finds and secreting it in purses or the folds of her gown, and she conquers hundreds of men. Reason temporarily protects her "foster-children," taking a mother's part, but Avarice goes a step further: she hides her greed and her monstrous appearance under a pious covering, the pretence of care for her children, or thrift (563). Avarice is the mother of crimes, Reason the foster-mother of virtues. Avarice's maternal appearance deceives the credulous hearts of men and they follow her once more. It is only Good Works (*Operatio*), who can defeat her; when she appears, Avarice is paralyzed by terror and puts up no struggle. Discord, too, acts in a deceptive, "feminine" way (her other name, she tells us, is Heresy), disguising herself as a friend, wounding Concord with a hidden weapon, and then giving herself away by her fear, her pallor and trembling.

We would expect the biblical examples cited for the virtues to be men, physically as well as morally, and indeed Job and David are praised, and Samuel is mentioned, but it is interesting that the human examples of victory over lust are both women. One is Judith, a successful warrior like the virtues of the poem, the other, Mary. Judith's cutting off the head of Holofernes (here lust is represented by a man) prefigures the power of earthly bodies to overcome lust, a power which the virgin birth brings to all men. After Mary, all flesh is divine which conceives God (76–77), which builds the temple to Wisdom in the soul. That is, by overcoming vice, man can bear Christ within his soul; he can become Mary and achieve the highest human feat—union with God.

Prudentius speaks at the end of his poem of the prison of the heart (*carcere cordis*, 906), meaning the bondage of the flesh from which the virtues must free the soul. Boethius begins the *Consolation* in that same prison, wrapped up in worldly concerns and self-pity, and it is from that prison, not the actual building which holds his body, that Philosophy, wisdom, struggles to free him in the course of the dialogue. Philosophy speaks of Boethius' attachment to worldy goods, fame, wealth, and position as the worship of Fortune, from whom she must win him back. Thus Boethius is also torn between two women representing two kinds of life. Fortune, however, never appears in the poem except in Philosophy's description, as a personification created by a personification. Philosophy herself is a projection of Boethius' mind. She appears at first as a separate figure against whom he argues and rebels, but which he eventually accepts as a part of himself; by the last books, he is raising the right questions to carry her arguments forward (from Book IV, ii). Fortune is a figure his mind creates; that is, man imagines Fortune as a real force so he can blame her for what he considers the random actions of fate. Eventually, Philosophy makes him see that Fortune is part of the workings of fate and not a separate and hostile entity, that it was his perspective that was wrong and not her actions. All that we know, she tells him in Bk. V, Pr. iv, ll. 75–77,[19] is known not by its own force but by our faculty of comprehension.

Boethius attacks Fortune for having betrayed him; he has willingly taken all she offered—wealth, honor, and success—but when she abandons him, when she acts according to her nature, he turns on her. First he had worshipped Fortune for being what she was, now he attacks her for not being what she is not. Fortune, as Philosophy describes her, is a capricious mistress whom men choose but cannot control; she plays with men to prove her power, practicing alluring familiarity with those she intends to deceive, but she is constant in her mutability (Bk. II, Pr. i and M. i). She is true to herself in her continual changing, and, on the downward swing of her wheel, when she abandons her followers, she is doing them the greatest good. Indeed,

---

[19] Boethius, *The Theological Tractates,* trans. by H. F. Stewart and E. K. Rand, Loeb Classical Library (1918; repr. Cambridge: Harvard University, 1962).

then she is doing Philosophy's work, for she teaches them, through adversity, the nature of true happiness (Bk. II, Pr. viii).

Boethius' error was to devote himself to her and to equally misleading women, the muses, who seem to represent the distracting and superficial beauties of the arts. Philosophy calls them theatrical harlots (*scenicas meretriculas,* Bk. I. Pr. i, 1. 29) and sirens, although she herself uses poetry and song as well as logic to persuade Boethius. She makes the classical distinction between art that is solely for amusement and art that is also for edification. The muses, she says, feed him on sugared poison; they kill the fruit of reason with the thorns of affections. In other words, they render his mind sterile and prevent it from conceiving as it was meant to do, by joining external shapes with internal forms (Bk. V, Pr. iv, 92 ff). Like Fortune, who feeds him on wealth, the muses only do him harm. Philosophy, however, nourishes him with virtue; *virtutum omnium nutrix,* Boethius calls her (Bk. II, Pr. iv, 1. 2). She is his physician and nurse, she wipes his tears with her gown, removing the veil of self-pity and forcing him to see himself as he is, and she persuades him by singing gently and softly, alternating her lessons with the delights of verse to refresh him. She plays several womanly roles, including the wise and firm mother/nurse, and the lovely, comforting companion. Everything Philosophy does is directed at freeing Boethius' mind, imprisoned more than his body by earthly ties, so that she (*mens,* the mind), can learn to despise earthly things and rise to heaven (Bk. II, Pr. vii). Philosophy gives her wings to ascend the skies, to return home (Bk. IV, Pr. i and M. i), to remember the truth she once knew despite the obstacle of the flesh, and finally to conceive and bring forth wisdom.

Mind is feminine because of the gender of *mens,* but she is a female figure and, because of her function, she is associated with Philosophy herself, the expression of Boethius' thought. In the story Philosophy uses to illustrate Boethius' position and to warn him of its dangers, she identifies his mind with Euridice.[20] Orpheus, whose wife

[20] Guillaume de Conches, in his commentary on the *Consolation,* interprets Euridice as natural desire, concupiscence, and *ingenium* (nature and cleverness), the latter being probably the closest to Boethius' meaning.

becomes the prisoner of Hell, of earthly desires, is Boethius. Boethius' mind has been given over to ambition and wealth, but it could be freed by the use of his divine gift, reason. Orpheus used his talent to move nature and the Gods to free Euridice, but when he looked back he lost her. This is what Boethius will do unless he heeds Philosophy's lesson and turns his back on Hell, on earthly concerns, once and for all. It is not Euridice, any more than Fortune, who draws him to destruction; the choice is his. If he chooses Philosophy, he will save Euridice. In her telling, Philosophy does not carry the story of Orpheus to its conclusion—Orpheus' death at the hands of the Bacchantes—but surely she means Boethius to know it, to realize that if he leaves his Euridice in Hell, all his talent will not save him; he will be torn apart by destructive and violent passions. But if he scorns the world, rejecting Fortune's riches for Philosophy's, he will free his mind, even though his body remains in prison.[21]

There is a twelfth-century allegorical dialogue based on the *Consolation* entitled *De eodem et diverso,* by Adelard of Bath, which embodies the opposition between the two ways of life in two women, Philosophia and Philocosmia.[22] The latter has certain obvious connections with Fortune, but she actually appears in the poem and voices her own arguments; the opposition which was implicit in Boethius is at the center of this work. Philocosmy appears with five women, servants who represent wealth, power, position, fame, and pleasure, and stands to the writer's left. Philosophy, accompanied by seven virgins, the liberal arts, stands on his right. Philocosmy points out the futility of philosophic investigation, the dependence of scholars on the senses which they scorn, and, most cutting, the desire of philosophers for her gifts—wealth and position—the very things they most vehemently attack. Philosophy answers that the soul is imprisoned in the body and

[21] In a subtle way, the marriage metaphor operates in this story through the analogy of Orpheus and Euridice to Boethius and his mind, and to Boethius and Philosophy. The marriage of Philosophy and the wise man is found in several twelfth-century references, as Wetherbee points out, p. 133.

[22] Ed. H. Willner, *Beitrage zur Geschichte der Philosophie und Theologie des Mittelalters,* Vol. 4, No. 1 (Münster, 1903).

can only free itself through learning, that it is made in the image of
God and can only fulfill itself when it is concerned not with things but
with causes. The author refuses Philocosmy's offer of gold and returns
to his studies, giving himself to Philosophy.

A similar opposition can be seen in Martianus Capella's *De
nuptiis Philologiae et Mercurii,* an early work to which Adelard and
the other twelfth century allegorists owe a great deal. Here the conflict
is between Venus and Pallas, the goddesses of love and wisdom.
Learning is the main subject of the poem, but the structure of the work
is neither a debate nor a battle; it is a pair of journeys leading to a marriage. The emphasis throughout is on balance and union rather than
opposition. Both the hero and the heroine make a journey, Mercury
down to earth to find a bride (Bk. I), Philology up to heaven for the
wedding (Bk. II). We actually have two heroes in this work, one male
and one female, both given equal attention, the two journeys balancing
one another. The celestial journey in the *De mundi* and the *Anticlaudian* will be made by a female figure, on the model of Martianus. Martianus, however, is making a point with the double journey: when he describes the litter in which Philology rides, he says it is
borne by two girls and two boys because Immortality ordered that *both
sexes* should be able to rise to heaven with Philology (Bk. II, §145).[23]

Marriage in this poem is also based on equality. When Mercury chooses a bride, Jupiter insists on taking her into the assembly of
the Gods so their marriage "may begin in equality as is fitting" (Bk.
I, §93). And marriage is the basic metaphor for the created universe
and for harmony among men. The poem begins with a hymn to Hymenaeus, the sacred principle of unity amongst the Gods, who binds
the warring seeds of the world with secret bonds and encourages the

---

[23] "Sic enim Athanasia praeceperat, ut uterque sexus cum Philologia coelum posset as-
cendere." *De Nuptiis Philologiae et Mercurii et de Septem Artibus Liberalium,* Libri
Novem (Frankfurt: Varrentrapp, 1836). An English translation was done by W. H.
Stahl, but so far only Vol. I, the Commentary, has appeared in Columbia Records of
Civilization (New York: Columbia University, 1971). I was able, however, to consult
the translation in manuscript, for which I am most grateful to Columbia Press.

union of opposites by his sacred embrace, who causes the elements to interact and make the world fertile, who brings harmony between the sexes and fosters loyalty through love. We can see this harmony operating on a "human" level among the Gods: Juno is able to persuade Jupiter to change his decrees by her embrace, and it is a power she uses, in this poem at any rate, for good. It is the reciprocal love among the Gods which inspires Mercury to find himself a bride in the first place.

Harmony is accomplished in this work through love; the figure of Harmony is Venus' daughter, and it is she who ends the marriage procession. Venus' number, six, the product of the male triad and the female dyad, is the source and origin of musical concords, hence Venus is said to be the mother of harmony (Bk. VII, §737). Music is itself a marriage of masculine rhythm (the result of "virile, form-producing activity"), with feminine melody (the matter on which form is imposed), (Bk. IX, §995). Together, rhythm and melody delight and move men: "ardor and song combine to delight our breasts," Harmony sings (Bk. IX, §917), "let us sing and let us love." It is no accident that the two creative processes of man, art and love, are combined here at the end of the poem, and that both offer pleasure and product.

Although Minerva (Pallas) and her followers, the liberal arts, are honored throughout the work, it is Venus' daughter Harmony and Venus' power to stir men's desires that prepares the consummation of the marriage. Throughout the poem, despite the heavy emphasis on learning, intellect and feeling are balanced. Venus is upset by the attention given the liberal arts at the wedding; she complains that Pallas usurps the rites that should be hers, that the Virgin goddess depresses nuptial spirits (Bk. VII, §725), that learned teachers thwart conjugal pleasures (Bk. IX, §888). She frequently expresses her boredom at the long speeches and her complaints are heeded—speeches are cut short or put off. Venus and her companions, Desire and Cupid, sometimes interrupt the ceremony, their high spirits causing them to break into laughter. The male Gods all respond to Venus' suggestive looks, flirting casually with her throughout the ceremonies—which even Juno tolerates, except when the groom becomes too fascinated. (He must, however, be susceptible to Venus if he is to see the marriage through.) Venus is the mother of all love and pleasure (*amorum voluptatumque mater omnium,* Bk. I, §85). Pallas (Minerva, Athena) is the bearer of all knowledge, intelligence, and perspicacity, the guiding genius of the universe (Bk. VI, §567), but she is also the patron of bloody warfare. She is called *virago,* as well as *virgo.* A masculine goddess, born of a father without a mother, she bears a shield because "wisdom rules the world or because the frenzy of battle looks to reason for succor" (Bk. VI, §569). Pallas has no interest in the proceedings; indeed, she feels out of place at a wedding. Martianus seems to be saying that Venus' affection and pleasure, and the harmony that result from them, are necessary to balance the harshness of the goddess of wisdom, just as the stability which Philology's learning brings to Mercury is necessary to balance the rashness of unenlightened intellect.[24]

In the union of Philology and Mercury we see the proper balance of contrasting natures. Medieval writers commonly take Mercury to represent Eloquence: Guillaume, in *De philosophia mundi,* mentions the marriage of Mercury and Philology and says that Mercury is speech (*sermo vel facundia*) and Philology is investigation; John of Salisbury, discussing this work in the *Metalogicon* (IV, xxix), calls Mercury the god of eloquence; Bernard Silvester, in his commentary on Martianus, says Mercury is speech (*sermo*) and Philology is reason (*ratio*).[25] But Mercury must be more than eloquence, for we are told that he had once been married to Eloquence (*Facundia*), whom Philology meets as she journeys to heaven (Bk. II, §172–73). Mercury appears to be creative intellect, the divine inspiration that enables man to use his knowledge, perhaps even the expression of the divine mind: "the faithful reflection and interpreter of my mind, sacred intelligence

[24] Cf. Guillaume de Conches, *De philosophia mundi,* who cites Cicero on the harm of eloquence without wisdom, a topos.

[25] Manuscript, Cambridge, University Library, Mm I, 18, 1r.

. . . through him I, the father, make my covenant,'' Jove says.[26] By her union with Mercury, Urania tells the bride, she who has studied the turning of the spheres will be able to determine the causes (Bk. II, §118); through their union, men will rise to heaven (II, 126). The power Mercury gives her, then, is the ability to translate her perceptions and her knowledge to principles and to deduce laws from those principles—to express her knowledge and build on it. What she offers him, presumably, is the tools for his intellect to work with. Before he came to her, he had gone through a number of other possible brides, none of them right for him. His first choice was Sophia, pure Wisdom, Athena's foster sister and, like her, devoted to virginity; that is, pure wisdom cannot unite itself to man. He then turns to Prophecy (Pronoea), but she has given herself to Apollo. His next choice, Psyche, who was carefully educated by the Gods, has been snatched from the company of Virtue and is held captive by Cupid; that is, the human soul is too susceptible to desires of the flesh. Finally, Mercury fixes on Philology, born of an ancient line, highly educated, who knows the movements of the heavens and the seas, who penetrates the secrets of knowledge and all that the Gods can foreknow (Bk. I, §22); she is earth-born, but destined to rise to the stars (I, 93). Before she can begin the journey, however, she must make herself ready for the wisdom of the heavens, free herself of the limited ideas of men; to do so, she literally vomits up all manner of writings (Bk. II, §135–36). These works of men are limited, but not valueless—the Arts and Disciplines go through what she has rejected, picking out what they need for themselves. Mercury has sent Philosophy, the love of wisdom, to guide Philology to heaven. Through Philosophy, we are told, Jupiter permits anyone to ascend to the heavens; that is, it is love of wisdom, not bits of knowledge, that lifts the mind to heaven. Once there, the groom bestows on her the seven liberal arts as her dowry, the dis-

[26] See Wetherbee, p. 87, and Stock, p. 93. Mercury is the means by which the divine plan is articulated—like Christ (though not a Christ figure), he is a medium between the creator and creation.

ciplines on which the structure of the universe and human knowledge
are based.[27]

Bernard Silvester, in his commentary on Martianus' poem,
connects Mercury's journey through the regions of the world (led by
Virtue), with Boethius' journey through false goods to the *summum
bonum* (led by Philosophy), and with Aeneas' journey through the Underworld (led by the Sibyl). In his commentary on the *Aeneid,* he says
that Aeneas is the human spirit and his journey to Italy is a quest for
self-knowledge (see Appendix). The quest for knowledge and the
quest for good are the same for Bernard, but his concern is less with
this quest and the union that is its goal, than with the union that
produces life. He speaks of the marriage of the Gods in *De nuptiis* as
the mutual nourishment of the elements of the world (*mutuum mun-
danorum alimentum*). The nuptial apparatus stems from the union of
opulence, Bacchus (*temporalis opulentia*) and desire, Venus (*voluptas
carnis*). Bacchus is the son of Jupiter and Semele, the earth, so his opulence is connected with the natural power of the earth to produce. As
Cupid, love, and Hymenaeus, marriage, are the offspring of Bacchus'
union with Venus, marriage is the result of natural abundance and the
desire to produce—union for procreation. Bernard uses the marriage
metaphor in his own allegory, *De mundi universitate,* in relation to the
life of the created universe and the human body: the soul is the bride,
the life force of the physical body, whether of man or of the world.[28]

[27] The presentation of the liberal arts makes up the bulk of the book, but since it offers
little that is unusual on the symbolism of women, I have passed over it in this chapter. I
should point out, however, that the liberal arts and the celestial journey are probably
more influential on later writers than the underlying concepts that I have been discussing
(the balancing of opposites, the equality of male and female, and the necessity of their
union to preserve life and order).

[28] Endelechia is called the bride (*sponsa*) of the world (*mundum*). Their contract is arranged by Providence, ''lest so glorious a bride should protest that the universe spawned
by mother Silva was an unworthy husband'' (I, ii, 180 ff). Providence fastens the body
of the universe to the soul as if it were glued or bound in marriage, thereby changing
hostility to favor, agreement to affection and faith. When man is created, the soul is
carefully prepared in heaven so that she may ''dwell as a queen in the earthly vessel'' of
the body (II, v), the husband seeming less glorious than his bride.

Through the sexual act, man becomes part of the process of creation, for reproduction is all that prevents the return to chaos which would undo the whole work of creation.[29] Heretofore in the allegories we have discussed, birth and conception have been used figuratively; here, human reproduction is important in itself. Bernard is concerned not with man's conquest of himself, but with the creation of the universe and man's place in it; his poem is an interpretation of the myth that so many twelfth-century writers struggled with—creation according to Plato's *Timaeus* without contradicting Genesis.

Instead of the traditional allegorical figures of virtues and vices, liberal arts and Philosophy, Bernard presents, for the first time in a major medieval poem, Natura and Noys. His Natura represents both human nature, after the creation of man, and the whole physical universe; Noys is the mind of God.[30] All the agencies of creation in this work, except God the Father, are female. Even those figures which are analogous, at least in function, to the second and third persons of the trinity are women. Bernard also associates women with the trinity in his commentary on Martianus, but there he is ascribing a Christian meaning to pagan goddesses: he compares Jove, Juno, and Pallas to the Christian trinity—Jove as the divine power, Juno as will, and Pallas as wisdom. This interpretation is not unique with Bernard (see Appendix), but the female members of the trinity in the *De mundi,* if we can so describe them, are unusual. In the poem, he is not only adopting the poetic tradition of personifying abstractions as women, but also drawing on the female ability to bring forth and nourish life. All the female figures in the *De mundi* have children or life-producing wombs. Noys, God's mind and roughly analogous to

[29] The sexual act, Wetherbee says, speaking of the end of the *De mundi,* reveals most strikingly the analogy between man's constitution and the orderly processes of the universe, p. 182 ff.

[30] On Natura in classical and medieval literature, see Economou. Noys is described in Macrobius as a personification but does not appear as a character. On Natura as human nature, see Stock, pp. 187 and 224: Nature, "representing the *causae primordiales* in the outside world, is internalized as *humana natura''*; See also Wetherbee, in the introduction to the *Cosmographia,* pp. 19 and 35.

the Logos or second person of the trinity, is the seed-bed of life; she calls Nature the blessed fecundity of my womb (*uteri mei beata fecunditas*, I, ii, ll. 3–4). Silva, the formless mass from which the elements are shaped, holds the original nature of things in her womb; as the mother of species, she conceives and gives birth to all, opening the womb of her fecundity to the production of life (I, ii, 96 ff); she is the inexhaustible womb of generation. Earth, *tellus*, is also spoken of as a loving mother, a womb. Some of the characters in the poem are more literally mothers, having given birth to other personifications: Noys is the mother of Nature, Urania, and Physis; Physis is the mother of Theory and Practice. Motherhood is so much a feature of the female in this poem that Venus is depicted with Cupid hanging from her left breast, an echo of the Virgin and the infant Christ (Bk. II, v, l. 184). Venus has her part in the continuing process of creation: she inspires the renewal of all creatures by the generative impulses and she draws forth fruits by the largesse of her own nature (II, v, 175 ff), just as Nature does when she visits earth (II, ix, 31 ff). But since creation works by a process of emanation from one stage to the next, each figure in the process is spoken of as female in relation to the next higher in the hierarchy, and male in relation to the lower. Noys, for example, is impregnated with the divine will, that is, she is female in relation to God, the creator, but Noys informs Endelechia, the world soul, with examples of the images she conceives, acting as the male in giving the forms. Endelechia, in turn, informs Nature, supplying the substance of souls, while Nature compounds the bodies in which the souls will dwell, just as in contemporary physiology, man gave the life and shape, woman the matter out of which the fetus was formed. Nature then informs Imarmene, temporal continuity (Bk. I, iv, 120 ff).

It is Nature who expresses the desire for the imposition of form, asking God to impose it on the formless mass of Silva. Silva, though she longs for form while she is still formless chaos (I, i, 18–22), is indifferent to good and evil; indeed, Bernard comments, malice preponderates in her (I, ii, 24–25). Her substance has the capacity to be transformed to a nobler state, but "rough necessity always lurks close beneath the surface'' (II, xiii, 17–28); that is, matter, as the Timaeus asserts, has a tendency to return to chaos. This tendency is held off by the male reproductive organs whose function is to insure the continuity of life—to impose individual form on formless matter— in a pale reflection of God's original act. The Oyarses, genius figures who dwell in every region of the heavens, are also a reflection of the male principle of reproduction; they assign forms to the lower world according to the heavenly pattern (II, iii, 91 ff and II, v, 46 and 76). Alanus will make much more of the need for male figures to regulate reproduction and impose order; Bernard is concerned with birth and the beginning of life and therefore concentrates more on the female figures. Since Bernard ends his work with the beginning of human history, he is not concerned with the dangers of lust. Alanus, on the other hand, who takes up after the fall, is preoccupied with the perversions of the sinful act. His aim is to conquer lust, to purify sex, and to restore man to his proper place within the natural order. In Alanus' poems, Venus represents lust and, in the *Anticlaudian,* she fights on the side of evil.

In his tractates, Alanus connects sex with sin in a conventional way: he says, in the *Summa Quoniam Homines,* that it is man's conception in lust that binds him to original sin (Bk. II, Tr. iv, 174). It is not surprising, therefore, that he is far more concerned with virginity than Bernard.[31] He exalts virginity as the highest state: it is the treasure of nature, once lost it does not return; it is the flower which, flowering, does not bloom again, the star which, falling, does not return, the gift which, lost, is not compensated. By this state alone, man can imitate angels and conquer himself (*Summa de arte praedicatoria,* XLVII). Alanus glorifies the Virgin in his interpretation of the Canticles (see above, pp. 29–30), and in his philosophical allegories vir-

---

[31] In *De arte praedicatoria,* Alanus says that marriage is good but the unmarried state is better, for in marriage one has two masters, God and the husband, and one cannot serve two masters (XLVI). Any who suggest marriage to those who prefer to remain virgins are people of confusion, of Babylon (''your father is the tinder of sin which engendered you, your mother's home is concupiscence'' XLVII).

gins dominate the imagery. In the *Anticlaudian,* Prudence enlists the
aid of a series of virgins, some of whom are, like the Virgin Mary,
mothers as well: Grammar (the first of the liberal arts and basic to all
as their means of expression) suckles an infant at her breast and brings
up the child, acting both as father, in correcting it, and as mother, in
feeding it (II, vii). Arithmetic (basic to the order of the universe, for
number binds all things) is mother and source, giving birth and mul-
tiplying herself; [32] she transcends man in mind, woman in sex. That
Virgins should dominate a poem concerned with reproduction may
seem odd, but, as Alanus reminds us, Christ came to create para-
doxes and the virgin birth is the ultimate paradox of creation (V, ix).
The created universe is built on the wedding of opposites and there is
no more perfect fusion of opposites than virgin and mother.

Alanus is interested in conception in an intellectual sense: a
mental marriage, he tells us, is enacted in the chamber of mind, where
concepts take form; mind, the mother, conceives, reason nourishes,
act brings forth (III, iv, §352). Only in the case of the Virgin Mary is
conception in the womb better than in the mind. In the *Summa q. h.,*
Alanus cites a passage from the Gospels (Luke 11:27–28), in which
Christ says just the opposite: responding to a woman who has blessed
the womb that bore Him, He comments "rather are they blessed who
hear the word of the Lord and keep it." To fulfill the word is to conceive in the mind; inasmuch as conception in the mind is the cause of
conception in the womb and a cause is better than its effect, mental
conception is higher than physical. However, conception of God in
the mind is common, but in the womb it is unique. The first may be
more useful, but the second is more glorious; hence the physical conception of the Virgin Mary, Alanus concludes, is higher than the mental conception of other men (Bk. I, Pt. i, 24). In the *De planctu Naturae,* Alanus attacks man for refusing to cooperate in physical con-

---

[32] On her robe is shown "quomodo Virgo parit, gignens manet integra, simplex sese
multiplicat" (III, iv). *Anticlaudianus,* ed. R. Bossuat (Paris: Vrin, 1955), also in PL,
120, 482–574.

ception, obstructing the work of Nature, and perverting her tools but he uses grammatical images for sexual perversion: Venus (lust) unmans men, makes the active passive, the predicate the subject. Even here, his approach to sex is abstract and intellectual (M.I., PL 120, 431).[33]

Alanus, being more interested in theory than in physical reproduction and more concerned with sin than Bernard, tends to play down the female figures in his poems, particularly in the *De planctu,* which is primarily concerned with what has gone wrong. His Nature is modeled on Boethius' Philosophy in that she comes to the poet from heaven when he is lamenting, dressed in a gown on which are pictured all living things, and her tunic is torn where man has committed unnatural acts against her. She has nourished the poet before and offers him medicine now to cure him of his illusions, using sweet words to bring him back to consciousness. She does have something to teach him, about his place in the natural order, but she is not Philosophy. She does not have the same rational powers, and she admits her own limitations in comparison to Theology: I walk the earth, she serves in heaven (PL, 431). Nature appears to the poet as a beautiful woman, according to literary convention, with golden hair, shining countenance, perfect proportions (PL, 432). Her beauty should move him to desire and thence to the work of procreation. He does succumb, at first, falling in ecstasy as she approaches (442), but instead of concentrating on her and his duty to her, he gets distracted by the subject of Cupid, who represents the self-centered and potentially destructive passion of literary tradition, precisely what the poet had complained of in other men. The poet is thus an illustration of the dichotomy between man's rational and physical nature—there is no connection between what he says and what he does.

Nature seems to possess many of the functions that Bernard assigned to other figures in the *De mundi,*[34] but she has failed in one

[33] The *De planctu* can also be found in *The Anglo-Latin Satirical Poets and Epigrammatists,* ed. T. Wright, Vol. II (1872; repr. Wiesbaden: Kraus, 1964).

[34] Endelechia, Imarmene, and Urania, according to Wetherbee, p. 188; the legitimate Venus, as well, according to Economou, p. 74 ff and particularly p. 85.

crucial function. Because she prefers to stay in the eternal regions, she has left the work of procreation on earth to Venus, that is, to the simple physical urge, without considering the dangers. Venus quickly tires of her duty, abandons her husband, Hymen (marriage), and lawful reproduction, and gives herself to Antigamus (Anti-marriage), to whom she bears a bastard son, Jocus (Sport). The problem is that sex for pleasure and no other purpose works against nature and life, against the continuation of species. Nature and Venus, the female figures connected with sex in this poem, cannot control man; they can only set his physical impulses in motion. This is apparently why Alanus introduces certain male characters—particularly Hymen, Nature's brother, and Genius, her son, as well as the unidentified man who drives Nature's chariot to regulate her course and "aid the weakness of her womanly nature" (PL, 439). The charioteer may, as Economou suggests, represent the ideal condition of man (which in the *Anticlaudian* will only be achieved with the aid of God and heavenly powers).[35] In any case, his presence makes it clear that the woman, Nature, cannot carry out her functions properly on her own.

Hymen and Genius represent rational, masculine control; at the same time, their existence reinforces the importance of the union of the sexes essential for preserving the established order. Hymen is the peacemaking unity, the inseparable yoke, the indissoluble bond of matrimony (PL, 472). There is no feminine softness in his face, just the authority of virile dignity. The virtues necessary to the moral life—Chastity, Temperance, Humility, etc.—are in *his* train, not Nature's. While Venus remains with him, while lust is contained within marriage, sex can function properly. Their son, Cupid (desire), though by no means ideal, can be made to serve Nature's purpose, while Venus' bastard, Jocus, cannot. Genius is Nature's son, but, like Christ in relation to the Virgin, he is a good deal more. Wetherbee suggests that Nature is a type of the church and that Genius, her priest, is the

---

[35] Economou, p. 77.

Word; [36] in fact, Alanus says that when Genius kisses Nature, the Eternal Word greets matter and Truth is born (PL, 480). He is Nature's alter ego, who gives form to her matter; he is her lover and her priest, and all the male-female relations in one, all chaste and all working in the cause of providence. It is he who must excommunicate man from Nature's order; Nature cannot do it herself, apparently because she is a woman, as *res,* even though as *signum* she is the vicar of God.[37] Genius' main function is to turn the images of things from the shadow of pictures to the truth of essence (479). He is what makes living things individuals. However, he is not perfect either, for only the source of creation, God, can be perfect; all other forms of creation, however high, are defective in some way. Genius draws virtues with his right hand but when he tires he uses his left, and then he produces vices. The *De planctu* leaves us with the sense that none of Nature's cohorts, whether male or female, can properly control man. What is needed is a rational control from within, the divinely created and anointed soul that will be sought in the *Anticlaudian.*

The perfect human whose creation is the subject of the *Anticlaudian* is, of course, a man, but the figures who create his body and soul are female. Alanus turns to intellectual and moral abstractions, rather than cosmological figures, to restore man to an ideal condition. Instead of relying on the physical side of human nature (Venus), Nature turns to the intellectual. Indeed she rejects lust (Venus appears in the poem only in the army of the vices) [38] and relies entirely on wisdom. Man's mind can do what his body cannot; it

---

[36] Wetherbee, p. 207. Genius "transmits Divine Wisdom into the sphere of Nature"; see Wetherbee, "The Function of Poetry in the *De planctu naturae* of Alain de de Lille," *Traditio* 25 (1969), 114. He is an intermediary between God and Nature.

[37] Economou discusses this explanation, and its limitations, on pp. 91–92.

[38] Venus is degraded progressively in the allegories—from her role in Martianus as essential to marriage and life, to the corrupted aide of Nature in the *De planctu* and the cohort of evil in the *Anticlaudian.* In the *Roman de la Rose,* she becomes a powerful figure of lust, who uses Nature and Genius to do *her* will.

can serve Nature's purpose without sin. It is Prudence who goes to heaven for the soul, accompanied by Reason in a chariot fashioned by the liberal arts. And it is Prudence who, with the help of Theology and Faith, obtains God's grace and receives the soul from Noys. All the characters involved in this journey except God, who is the object of it, are women. All the aspects of human wisdom and learning, and even divine wisdom as it is perceived by man (Noys), are female. The journey Prudence makes is a reverse of creation: she proceeds upwards from earth through the visible universe, back to ideal forms and, finally, to the cause of all, God. For man's mind, of course, this is the forward journey: he begins with the senses and the liberal arts, human learning, proceeds via Theology to Faith, and, finally, in Faith's mirror, he is able to see the first causes.

For this poem, Alanus draws on all the major allegories we have discussed in this chapter, on Prudentius for the battle of virtues and vices, on Boethius' Philosophy for the figure of Prudence, on Martianus for the liberal arts, and on Bernard for Noys and Natura and the journey to God. He brings all these sources together to show that man must use every intellectual tool, all the products of the human mind, along with the divine gifts of faith and doctrine, to be restored, to become what he was meant to be. This point is emphasized in the figure of Prudence, who has a variety of names, Phronesis, Sophia, Minerva, because she is Wisdom in whatever form man knows it. She too resembles Boethius' Philosophy (her head is sometimes in the heavens, she mounts to heaven and descends to earth, and her dress is torn) and like Philosophy her function in man is to teach him his place in the providential order. She does not, however, appear to man to carry out this function, as Philosophy does in the *Consolation,* or Nature in the *De planctu* (the latter only to fail). In the *Anticlaudian,* her preparation of man is far more abstract; it is only by reconstructing the steps of her journey up and back as they occur within man's mind that we see the full analogy with Boethius. The figure of Nature in the *Anticlaudian* still has great powers: she designs laws, examines the causes of things and the origins of the world (I, v); it is she who

redeemed ancient chaos, who imposed the kiss of peace on the elements. But within the poem, she plays a small role: she suggests the
journey and provides the body to house the souls Prudence brings from
heaven, but it is Prudence's journey that matters.

The soul is fashioned in heaven, by God, through Noys, while
the body is made on earth. The body is male because it must be
married to the soul, but also because it must be morally strong, virile.
That is, moral weakness is equated with effeminacy: e.g., Moderation
prevents the ideal man from indulging in female extravagances (*fe-
mineos luxus*) of dress and grooming; Piety teaches him to be flexible
and charitable, but not to be soft and effeminate, not to let his mind
lose its manly vigor (VII, vi); and Reason keeps a watchful eye on
Fortune to make sure her gifts will not lead the soul to vice or make
the mind's acts effeminate (VIII, ii). However, the female soul is
purer than the body it inhabits; Alanus points out that the body must
be carefully formed, a "suitable marriage bed must be found for the
spirit lest the corruption of the host infect the guest" (VI, vii). The
soul is a pilgrim on earth, a heavenly spirit that can travel here only in
the body and is put in the body to guide it back to God. In other
words, the female soul is purer than the masculine body it inhabits,
but when the body's corruptions are described, they are called "effeminate." This is an interesting clash of two conventions: the Neo-Platonic marriage of opposites, of body and soul, in which the female is
life-giving, against the moral, exegetic identification of woman with
vice. It is almost as if Alanus rejected women morally but accepted
them philosophically, as abstractions.

Alanus uses the female figures in this poem in a way that
recalls Prudentius and the moral allegory tradition; they are seen as opposing forces at work in man's nature. They are either forces for good
(Reason, Wisdom, Theology, the arts, and the various virtues), or
forces for evil (Alecto and the vices, including Venus). Something of
this can be seen in the *De planctu,* where the vices do not appear, but
are described in contrast to the virtues in Hymen's train. The vices are
spoken of as perversions of female roles, as nurses of discord, sisters

of madness, mothers of intemperance (463), whereas the virtues are
presented as virgins and dignified matrons. A similar opposition is
found in the seats of Nature and of Fortune in the *Anticlaudian:* Fortune's home is a rock in the sea, Nature's is in the center of a grove on
a mountain; Fortune's realm alternates between winter and spring, ste-
rility and fertility, Nature's knows no season and is perpetually flowering; Fortune's realm has two rivers from different sources, one sweet,
one bitter, Nature's has one fountain that enriches the soil.[39] Clearly
the contrast here is between worldly goods and natural goods, as in
Boethius' contrast of Philosophy and Fortune. Alanus' ideal man conquers the evil traits that try to control him, the vices in Alecto's army,
and thus renders himself impervious to Fortune's power. He is able to
do this because he is in perfect balance, a marriage of natural and
divine elements, of body and soul, earth and heaven, male strength
and female goodness.

For the symbolic life of women in medieval literature, the allegorical tradition presents several important concepts: the union of opposites as the basic principle of life; the need for the female as well as
the male in the order of things; the identification of the female with
good qualities, with the higher parts of human nature; and the presentation of women not only as forces for evil, seducing man into sin, but
also as forces for good, leading him upwards to virtue. In this chapter,
we have seen a sympathetic portrayal of women only in personified
abstractions; in the next, we will see it in human beings.

[39] According to H. R. Patch, *The Goddess Fortuna in Mediaeval Literature* (Cambridge: Harvard University, 1927), the homes of both Nature and Fortune borrow details
from Venus' home in Claudian. Patch notes similarities in the figures of Venus and Fortune in medieval tradition, and certainly Alanus sees aspects of Venus in both Fortune
and Nature.

Chapter Three

Courtly Literature

In the preceding chapters, we have seen historical and fictional women treated as abstractions and abstractions personified as women. In courtly literature we find a confusion of the two—a setting of courtship or marriage which would seem to demand a real woman, but more often yields a symbol. Lyric and romance poets are concerned with the effect of love on the man, his development of self-awareness and the ensuing inner conflicts. Love can provide a man with a new and nobler identity and inspire him to great deeds in the service of others, or it can cause a madness that cuts him off from his world and drives him into exile or death. The acknowledgment of love brings with it a series of conflicts for the lover, not only the moral conflicts we have seen in allegory, between good and evil forces, but also those of clashing moods and aspirations which he must learn to bring into balance. In the lyric, which describes emotional states, the lover alternates between hope and despair, desire and frustration, resignation and resentment; in romance, where the love is part of a narrative, the lover is faced by conflicting demands of chivalry and love, of society and personal desire, of worldly reputation and personal integrity. There is something of a psychomachia in these conflicts: the battle seems to be turned outwards, against other people, but the hero's enemies often reflect aspects of his problem. His life is a series of battles to overcome the evil forces which threaten the good. In lyric poetry, the battle occurs only as a metaphor, but the court setting provides hostile characters on whom the lover can project his own conflicting desires: the *lauzenger,* the scandalmongers, express the straightforward lust and the cynical doubts about love that he often feels but strives to overcome.

The force of love that creates conflicts in the lover operates through the lady. It is embodied in her to such an extent that she seems to be a personification of love. In the lyric, love and the lady are virtually interchangeable: they have the same powers and the same effect on the lovers; the same images and pronouns are used for both, making it impossible at times to tell which is meant. This is an intentional confusion, because it is one the poet feels. He selects the lady he loves or, to put it another way, he incarnates Love in a lady. Then he forms an image of her in his mind, attributes the qualities he values to that image, and worships or berates it, depending on his mood. The romance lady appears to be a separate being, but we will see that she is often a mirror image of the lover, or a figure he has somehow fashioned to his desires. Sometimes she is the force behind the action, drawing him to her with magic (for love is a force beyond his control) exerting an attraction that holds him despite family or lord. In some romances, there is a second woman who represents, as in allegory, a counter-impulse, either the hero's reason, working to control his fate (she may help him achieve a suitable union with his love) or the lure of the world, of chivalry and fame (she tries to keep him from his love). I will restrict my discussion in this chapter to early Provençal lyric poets and to French romances, because they are the earliest examples in their genres and are influential for later writers, and because I find them the most interesting for this study.[1]

The lyric lady is a kind of super-personification, the source and

[1] German and French lyric poetry of the late twelfth and early thirteenth centuries share many of the characteristics of Provençal poetry, e.g., the aloofness of the lady, and the preoccupation with the idea of love rather than with the individual object of it. German romances are more concerned than their French counterparts with preserving chivalric values and the social order, so they emphasize marriage and mutual love as the basis of social harmony. (This is particularly true of Hartmann and Wolfram, not of Gottfried.) To do so, however, they must make the women less forceful, e.g., Cundwiramur in Wolfram's *Parzival,* whose name suggests far greater significance than her part in the romance bears out.

repository of all good qualities. She is an ideal being the poet adores, but she is also a real woman whom the poet wishes to possess, because his love is both sexual desire that seeks fulfillment in bed [2] and mental yearning that finds its satisfaction in contemplating the image it has formed. Conversely, the personification of Love that appears in the poems (*Amors*) is described and treated as a real woman, alternately praised and condemned, cajoled and berated. What the poet worships, in fact, is *Amors,* the abstraction projected onto a real woman. We have moved one step beyond the worship of Philosophia, Natura, or Venus, with the introduction of a real woman. In her the poet can confront his emotions, the real conflicts between higher and lower impulses. One may be overwhelmed by the beauty of a personified abstraction, but with an abstraction one does not have to cope with the physical cravings that real bodies cause. On the other hand, if one wishes to accept those cravings and at the same time raise them above the lowest level, one has to seek a reality beyond the body.

The woman the poet loves is a mirror in which he sees his ideal self, what he might be.[3] How he sees her depends on how he feels or

---

[2] Love may be *joi,* an exaltation of spirit, but it is rarely free of sexual desire. Guillaume begins one poem with *amor, joy, joven,* and ends with a contrast between two horses, representing two kinds of woman, one fierce and untameable, the other agreeable [*Les Chansons de Guillaume IX,* ed. A. Jeanroy *Classiques français du moyen âge,* 2nd ed. rev. (Paris: Champion, 1964), 1]. (Henceforth references to the poems will be given in the text, the arab numeral giving the number of the poem in the cited edition, the roman numeral referring to the stanza of the poem.) Bertran de Born claims to love only the thought of his lady, but adds that if he ever fails her in that thought, he wants his companion, his sexual organs, to fail him when he is alone with her [*Die Lieder Bertrans von Born,* ed. C. Appel (Halle: Niemeyer, 1932) 4, ii–iii]. Most poets dream of seeing their ladies naked in their bedrooms, some have already achieved it. Sexual desires are often expressed in poems that begin with the mating of birds: Jaufré Rudel in *Les Chansons de Jaufré Rudel,* ed. A. Jeanroy *CFMA,* 2nd ed. rev. (Paris: Champion, 1965), 1, i; Marcabrun in *Poésies Complètes du Troubadour Marcabru,* ed. J. M. L. Dejeanne (Toulouse: E. Privat, 1909), 11, i. Arnaut Daniel compares the birds with their mates to lovers with "amigas en cui entendem" [*Arnaut Daniel, Canzoni,* ed. G. Toja (Firenze: Sansoni, 1960), 12, i]. The verb *entendem* suggests the harmony of spirits that distinguishes *fin'amor,* however physical it may be, from *fals'amor.*

[3] See Frederick Goldin, *The Mirror of Narcissus in the Courtly Love Lyric* (Ithaca: Cornell University, 1967), for an intensive study of the mirror image and its implications in

how he thinks she is treating him. If his mood is one of joy or hope, he may rise to hyperbolic praise and describe her as a godlike good who lights the world. He may even pretend to confuse her with God: holding her, Raimbaut d'Orange says, he feels he holds God (22, ii); her smile seems the smile of God (35, v); Peire Vidal thinks he sees God, when he looks at her lovely body (43, vi). There are dangers, however, in her excellence: Bernart de Ventadorn is afraid that if his lady becomes aware of her own value, his enemies, the slanderers, will turn her against him (13, iv).[4] This means either that if she recognizes her own value she will see how inferior he is and will give him up, or that, inasmuch as she represents his higher aspirations, if he strives too high he will recognize the futility of his quest for perfection and surrender to his worst self.

That the praise or blame is all a matter of his perspective is illustrated by a poem of Raimbaut's in which, in an attempt to win the lady's mercy, he tells her: don't believe your mirror—you are black and ugly (23, l. 119 ff). What he is saying is, "I am your mirror, not the glass; if you are not kind to me you are ugly because that is how I see you, and how I describe you." If the lady rejects the lover or, worse, turns to someone else, she is a *trichairitz,* a treacherous deceiver, lustful and inconstant. The excessive lust of some women is excused because the jealousy of their husbands drove them to it, but most women are condemned because it is their nature to be lustful.[5]

When his lady fails him, the poet often threatens to leave her for another who will be more receptive, but all the ladies are the same.

medieval lyric. Christiane Leube-Fey, *Bild und Funktion der dompna in der Lyrik des Trobadors* (Heidelberg: Carl Winter, 1971), notes that there are no realistic descriptions of the courtly lady in *canzones,* p. 38, and that the presentation of the *dompna* in provençal lyric is a continual attempt to define the ideal human being, p. 147.

[4] Raimbaut: *The Life and Works of the Troubadour Raimbaut d'Orange,* ed. W. T. Pattison (Minneapolis: Univ. of Minnesota, 1952); Peire Vidal, *Poesie,* ed. D'Arco Silvio Avalle, 2 vol. (Milano: Ricciardi, 1960); Bernard de Ventadour, *Chansons d'Amour,* ed. M. Lazar (Paris: Klincksieck, 1966).

[5] On the jealous husbands see Guillaume, 2, and Marcabrun, 2, v; on the nature of women see Guillaume, 5, and Marcabrun, 44.

Only his image of her, or perhaps his name for her, changes. Bertran de Born tells us that one who exchanges good for better (bo per melhor ... melhz) should be worth more. He has served *Melhz,* but she betrayed him. Now *Melhz-de-bè* ("better than good," or "better still") has come along and will give him her love; *she* will have as her lover one who knows how to be most worthy (3). He suggests, not very subtly through the senhals, that he is the best, that as his lady increases in worth, so does he, but since her worth depends on her receptiveness to him, the message to the first lady is that she must not reject him if she would remain worthy.

Whether it is good or bad, the image of the lady exists in the poet's mind and not in the world around him. For the most part, we are told little about any one lady that might distinguish her from another. She is almost always *bela, doussa, fina, genta,* filled with *pretz, sabers, cortezia, umiltatz;* she has beautiful eyes, white breasts, etc. Even when the poet offers details, like names, that suggest real women—and that is rare—they turn out to be allegorical, e.g., Peire Vidal, 35. The poet claims to hold certain fiefs through his lady, who appears to be wealthy (more than a hundred castles and three cities serve her). But if we look at the names of the fiefs, *Vertfuelh* and *Monlaur,* green flower and mount laurel, we see that another interpretation is possible; it is spring, youth, that he holds through her. And so on through the poem: she retains *Mongalhart* and *Daurabell,* boldness and golden beauty; she does not sell or mortgage *Beljoc,* the lovely game, that is, her love; she has him hold *Montamat* and *Bon Repaus,* beloved mount and good rest, "per melhs jazer," in order to lie better, that is, to make love.[6]

---

[6] There are some possible exceptions to this: Giraut de Borneil [*Sämtliche Lieder des Trobadors Giraut de Bornelh,* ed. A. Kolsen, 2 vol. (Halle: Niemeyer, 1910, 1935), 34], an envoi to a countess who holds Provence, through whom Savoy and Lombardy are enriched; Bertran de Born, 7 and 8, which may be dedicated to Matilda, sister of Richard I of England. But there is little in the poems to identify the lady, and much hyperbole (e.g., she is of high lineage and royal, so superior to others that the Roman crown would be honored if it encircled her head; she could choose from the bravest or richest barons).

From the earliest poets, we have spoofs of the unreal nature of this kind of love:

> Amigu'ai ieu, no sai qui s'es
> qu'anc non la vi
>
> . . . .
> Anc non la vi et am la fort

[Guillaume, 4, v and vi]

> I have a love, I don't know who she is
> for I've never seen her
>
> . . . .
> I've never seen her and I love her fiercely

(Cf. Jaufré, 6, *No sap chantar qui so non di.*) Bertran de Born plays with the idea of the perfect lady as a composite of all the desirable qualities a woman can possess (5). When his lady sends him away, he says he can love no other, for she has no equal. So, until he can win her back, he substitutes a "donna soisseubuda," a composite lady he constructs for himself by taking the best features of all the ladies he knows. But however artificial the love may be in one sense, it still has a powerful effect on the poet and, in that sense, it is very real. *Fin'amors* (true love), as opposed to *fals'amors* (possessive, cupidinous love), has the power to make the lover better, to inspire him to joy and song. "Ja non creirai ... hom per Amor no meillur," Marcabrun claims (13, iv: I will never believe that a man does not grow better through love), and Marcabrun is one of the fiercest critics of bad women.

Love and the lady both inspire the poet to sing, apparently indiscriminately: Peire d'Alvernha, in one poem, says that Love gave him the gift of being better at *trobar* (5, vi–vii), and in another, he says that if he did not love the lady so, he would not know how to make verse or melody (4, vii).[7] Sometimes they work together to inspire him (Love plains and gilds my song, which is inspired by her who rules and preserves worth; Arnaut Daniel, 10), and sometimes to wound him. Peire Vidal complains to Love and to the lady in the same

---

[7] Peire d'Alvernha, *Liriche,* ed. Alberto del Monte (Turin: Loescher-Chiantore, 1955).

words that he is near death because of them, and that it will be a sin if
they do not save him (to Love: 13, i; to Lady: 38, ii; 42, ii; 37, iii.).
Raimbaut speaks of Love and the lady as his two enemies; he would
fight Love because she has wounded him, but he does not know where
she is (23, 1. 27 ff). That is, despite the wounds she inflicts, Love is
not a real being. Occasionally the poet admits that the figure he blames
for all his trouble does not exist: Love has shown me only shame, indifference, Bernart de Ventadorn complains, I would do violence to
her if I could, but God did not want Love to be a creature (*res*) one
could take vengeance on with a sword, therefore I reject her and leave
the lady (33, iv).

Perhaps the poets speak of Love as a woman in order to shift
some of the blame from their ladies to an abstraction, just as they in-
carnate the abstraction in a lady in order to make the love more perfect. The figure of Love is a woman in Provençal partly because
Amors is a feminine noun,[8] but clearly also because the poets think of
Love and the lady as one. They had the classical model of Cupid, as
well as Venus, to draw on had they wanted a male figure.[9] Love's
powers do not differ perceptibly from the woman's: she can be a capricious tyrant, preferring the proud and faithless, perversely choosing
the worst suitor; she is cruel to those in her power; she uses the beauty
of the woman to make the poet her slave. A man under Love's rule
must follow her desires, "run where she wishes," Peire Vidal says
(39, i). But like the lady, Love can also be beneficent: Love brought
me to a castle, Arnaut relates, gave me dominion without tribute, and
there I found Instruction and Loyalty; Joy lifts my heart to the sky,
Love and Joy guide my heart (5, ii).

Amors is not the only personification that appears in Provençal

---

[8] German *Minne* and French *Amors* are also feminine, though the male *dieus d'amor*
often appears in French poetry. In Italian, Amore is masculine and the personified figure
is always a man who may use the lady as his tool but is not to be confused with her. See
below, p. 127.

[9] Raimbaut, 10, iv, is probably referring to Cupid when he speaks of "un traichor mal
fizel."

poetry, as the last reference indicates. *Joys, Joven, and Proeza* are common figures, sometimes united in family groups.[10] Allegorical thought is clearly not alien to Provençal poets; even when they are not using personifications, there is something allegorical in the love situation. The poet is always going through a kind of psychomachia between his higher and lower impulses. The lower inpulses are represented by the *lauzenger,* who are concerned only with sex and physical satisfaction, for whom a woman is nothing more than an object,[11] while the lady represents the higher aspirations, the striving for nobility, honor, valor, good. The *lauzenger* do not understand *fin'amor* and reduce all they see to their own vulgar terms. Everything is dirty in their eyes: when the poet manages to steal a kiss from his lady, he must hide it from them because they would distort its meaning (see Arnaut Daniel, 12, iii). Because they fail to comprehend the spiritual aspect of the love, they see the physical only in the most limited way. Since the goal of love is, in one sense, the same for them and for the poet—that is, sexual union—it is the path to that end and his attitude towards love and the lady that distinguishes the poet from them. When the poet succumbs to his lower impulses, he speaks like the *lauzenger* and accuses the lady of being fickle, treacherous, and selfish because she does not grant what he desires; when he is governed by the higher impulses, he asks only to be worthy of her, to be

[10] See Marcabrun: while *Jovens* was father of the world and *Fin'Amors* mother, *Proeza* was maintained, but now *Jovens* kills himself because *Amors* is lost and *Joi* disinherited (5, vi); there is no more comfort in Joven—cowards have thrown him out for his mother's fault (who the mother is is not clear) (9, iv); cf. 11, ii–iv, and 17, ii. These and other personifications appear often in Marcabrun's poems; see particularly 4, 15, 19, 21, 27, and 36. In the work of other poets, see Bernart de Ventadorn, 11, i; Peire d'Alverhna, 15, ii; Giraut de Borneil, 50; Peire Vidal, 4, vi and 6, i.

[11] There is a related group, the *gilos,* who represent the possessiveness and selfishness which make love impossible. They guard women as possessions, forcing them to seek lovers wherever they can find them. Poets condemn them and take care to dissociate themselves from them: "I never kept a cousin or female relation of mine from love," Raimbaut claims, 15, v–vi. [On the *lauzenger* and *gilos* in relation to the poet, see F. Goldin, "The Array of Perspectives in the Early Courtly Love Lyric," *In Pursuit of Perfection,* ed. J. M. Ferrante and G. D. Economou (New York: Kennikat, 1975).]

allowed to serve her and better himself in the service. Sometimes, in a debate with a friend, the poet speaks for the anti-love forces in his own voice. The friend may be thought of as the poet's other voice, even though he is ostensibly another poet, since what he says in defence of love often echoes the poet's words from other poems.[12] Giraut presents the debate with himself more directly in the form of questions and answers about his conflicting attitudes (21). Some poets use the language of war to describe the conflict: Marcabrun, "whoever gets involved in false love, makes war against himself" (37, iii); Bernart de Ventadorn, "Love conquers me with force and battle" (21, i); Peire d'Alvernha describes the lover as a captive in a castle where he is afraid to remain but cannot help defending himself against his enemies (9, iii); Giraut describes his heart, his sense, and his fear as fighting among themselves over whether to be angry with the lady (45).

The conflict in the lyric lover is between the right and wrong kind of love (*fin'amor* and *fals'amor*), devotion and lust. The woman, for the most part, represents the right love, the impulse that makes the man act nobly and inspires him to write poetry that will, ideally, move others to follow his example. The force of that love is embodied in the woman. In romance, too, the force of love is embodied in a woman who is the man's other self, who represents that part of him that can be inspired by deep feeling to do great deeds or to rise above the limitations of his world. "Love," in Hanning's words, "plays a special role in the attainment of self-awareness in romance. . . . Since the end of love is to make a new 'person' out of two previously separated selves, the outer adventures of the love quest function concurrently as a metaphor for the self's great inner adventure: its quest is to become the image it has generated of its own triumphant perfection." [13]

The romance hero falls in love with his own image (*Narcissus*

---

[12] See Marcabrun, 6, and Bernart de Ventadorn, 28 and 32.

[13] R. W. Hanning, "The Social Significance of Twelfth-Century Chivalric Romance," *Medievalia et Humanistica,* New Series, 3 (1972), 11–12.

is an extreme statement of the psychological reality), in the person of a woman who is a mirror image of himself (as in *Piramus et Tisbé* and *Floire et Blancheflor*), or one that he has, in a sense, created (as in *Tristan* and *Lanval*). Until he falls in love, until the woman intrudes herself on his life and awakens him to an aspect of his being he had not been aware of, his life has no apparent direction. Love means a rebirth; it awakens the hero to a new sense of himself, inspiring him not so much to greater deeds as to a higher purpose and responsibility. It reveals qualities in the hero which the lady sees and which the world often does not, but love also enhances those qualities. The lady could not love him if he were not worthy, but he is to some extent worthy because she loves him. Her presence in his life symbolizes his potential excellence. His final union with her (if he can achieve it) represents the completion of himself.

The woman is usually the first to feel love, the first to express it, and the instigator of the action that leads to its consummation. Because she represents a force that the man does not completely understand and cannot control, the lady is often said to possess supernatural powers—the power to cure fatal wounds or protect him from harm, to appear when needed or draw him to her. But this magic, which seems to give her control over his destiny, does not work forever; when he betrays his love in some way, he frees himself of that power and loses its benefits. Perhaps it is when he possesses her that she loses her power and then the fate of the love depends on him. Their love is often consummated in a strange land, or other world, which offers a new life to the hero, and which attracts him, but to which he cannot totally commit himself. He is drawn back to the old life by personal and chivalric ties or habits. The very activity which, in many cases, has won her—fighting—takes him away from her or sets up conflicts with his commitment to her which he is unable to resolve. In attempting to discharge his old responsibilities, he sometimes incurs new ones and finds himself caught between two women who have strong claims on him. The choice between the two women dramatizes the conflict inside the hero between the world and love; he is divided against himself, not sure of his own identity, unwilling to relinquish the old and unable to yield completely to the new. Sometimes his own doubts make him vulnerable to the second lady, which only intensifies his problem with the first (as in *Tristan* and *Ille et Galeron*). Sometimes the hero's fate is in the hands of two women working towards the same goal, but in different ways, one his love, the other a friend. When the love is offended and withdraws in anger, the friend offers comfort and, more important, counsel—stratagems to win back the lady. This second lady also represents a force within the lover, his reason; when she is involved in the action, his mind is working to control his fate, counterbalancing the emotion to which his will has surrendered. With her help, the lover wins back his love and achieves the reintegration of his personality—a harmony of love and reason.

These variations on woman as love can be traced through a number of late twelfth- and early thirteenth-century French romances, beginning with *Narcissus*. Through the story of a man who scorns the love of woman and then falls in love with his own image, the author shows the need for mutual love. He presents two kinds of love: one in the hero, a love that is completely self-absorbed and ultimately self-destructive; the other in the heroine, Dané, a love that seeks fulfillment in another being, and that might have saved the hero had he given in to it. But Narcissus is not capable of love because he lacks compassion. When Dané throws off her cloak, revealing both the beauty of her body and the suffering she has endured to find him, he is moved neither by desire nor by pity. His failure to feel any emotion for her is what condemns him; and, by denying her, he destroys himself.

The difference between the two kinds of love can be seen in the reactions of the two characters to one another and to the emotion they begin to feel. When Dané sees Narcissus, she is wounded by love; she recognizes the feeling quickly and accepts love's power over her. Though she is inhibited at first by a sense of responsibility to her father, the king, and by her fear of Narcissus' reaction, she decides to

force the issue and speak to him. Divided between her love and her
position, she is uncertain of her identity: *ses tu que soies fille a roi?*
(385: Don't you know you are the daughter of a king?) [14] she asks
herself. But after her first unhappy meeting with Narcissus, she accepts the new identity completely. Love has cut her off from the old
life, from her family:

> Qui sui je donc? Qui est mes pere?
> Li rois est ...
> . . . .
> Mençongne est! Ains sui orfeline:
> Je n'ai ami, je n'ai parent
>
> [599–603]
>
> Who am I then? Who is my father?
> He is the king. . .
> . . . .
> That's a lie! I am an orphan:
> I have no friends, I have no relatives.

She does not understand love (*qu'est Amors? Lasse/ Ne sai* [611–12]),
but she knows she cannot resist it and she turns to Venus and her son
for help, asking them to teach Narcissus what love is. They answer her
prayer, but Narcissus is too self-centered to love anyone but himself.
His vanity is apparent both when Dané first appears to him and when
he sees his own image in the fountain. He assumes, from the early
hour and her beauty, that she is a goddess or a fairy (454); as long as
he thinks she is a supernatural being, he is willing to speak with her,
but as soon as he discovers she is only a girl in love with him, he is
cold and cruel. Any baron, prince, or emperor would have wept at the
sight of her bleeding feet and weeping eyes, the poet comments, but
Narcissus leaves without listening to her. Later, when he looks in the
fountain, he thinks again that he sees a fairy, nymph, or goddess
(685–86), as if no mortal were worthy of his affection. He deceives
himself, the poet remarks (674). When he finally recognizes the
image, he despairs:

[14] *Narcissus, poéme du XIIe siècle,* ed. M. M. Pelan and N. C. W. Spence (Paris: Les
Belles Lettres, 1964).

Je sui ce que je tant desir
jou meismes me fas languir

[915–16]

I am what I so desire
I am the cause of my own distress.

He knows that to fulfill love there must be two and that the one he loves cannot help him; this is doubly true, not only because it is an image of himself that he loves, but because the self it is an image of has refused to give precisely that kind of help to another. He cannot love Dané even to save himself because he cannot get beyond self-love, so he destroys not only himself but Dané, the capacity to love another.

The self-destructive nature of such love can be mitigated by the projection of the lover's image onto a woman, but the tragedy cannot necessarily be avoided; the lover cannot always move beyond the satisfaction of his own desires. In both *Piramus* and *Floire,* the heroine is the mirror image of the hero. In the first, the romance ends with the death of both lovers, and in the second, with his conversion and their marriage. The lovers in *Piramus* are the children of neighbors; they are "d'une biautez et d'uns samblans" (6: one in beauty and in features).[15] As children, they are inseparable, their identity reinforced by a common upbringing until a servant alerts the girl's mother to their growing affection. Years later, despite an enforced separation, their love asserts itself and it is the woman through whom the love operates. It is she who finds the crack in the wall through which they speak, she who suggests the rendezvous. The strongest indication that she represents the impulse to love in Piramus can be found in the source of her plan for their meeting: she has had a dream of Piramus saying, "Come with me, the Gods tell us to leave the city to be together." In other words, she expresses Piramus' thought and desire. When the plan misfires because of the lion, Piramus kills himself; like Narcissus, he despairs too soon that he cannot fulfill his love. Like Dané, Tisbé dies

---

[15] *Piramus et Tisbé, poéme du XIIe siècle,* ed. C. de Boer, *CFMA* (Paris: Champion, 1921).

over her lover's body, killing herself with his weapon. In this tale, the lovers are made one by nature and by choice, but they are separated by external factors—their families and the lion. Their love is stronger than the circumstances that keep them apart, even than death, yet it cannot overcome the problems of life.

Floire and Blancheflor are similarly one by nature and by choice. The mirror image is even stronger in this romance than in *Piramus:* the two children are begotten on the same night, born on the same day, Palm Sunday, and named for that day, although he is pagan and she a Christian. They are cared for by the same woman, they live together and study together; they are alike in beauty and learning. When they are separated, and the girl is sent away, it is their physical resemblance that leads the boy to her. At every stage of his journey, strangers note the resemblance and send him after her. When he finds her, in a harem, the similarity leads to an interesting confusion. Hiding in her room, he is mistaken for a girl. In other words, the identity of the two is so strong that even sexual distinctions are blurred.

The strength of their love, which has not only drawn them together despite all the obstacles life or the romance could put between them, and which has made each willing to die in order to save the other, also moves the emir to pardon them. The love thus endangers them but also saves their lives and, what is more, saves Floire's soul—he becomes a Christian when he marries Blancheflor. Conventional as such a conversion may be at the end of a tale about a pagan and a Christian, it is still significant that the impulse to love that draws Floire to Blancheflor also leads him to God.

An identity of lovers so strong that one can be mistaken for the other may also be manifest in an exchange of roles. In *Aucassin et Nicolete* and in *Erec et Enide,* the man is so wrapped up in his love that he takes on the characteristics of a woman, or at least fails to act like a man. In *Aucassin,* the lovers are described in similar, if conventional, terms at the beginning.[16] However, once they are separated, the

---

[16] Aucassin: "caiax blons et menus et recerceles et les ex vairs et rians et le face clere et traitice et le nes haut et bien assis" (2); Nicolete: "les caviaux blons et menus recerceles

two act in very different ways. Nicolete, like Dané and Tisbé, becomes the active figure: she finds a way to escape from her prison and join her lover and eventually, after another separation, to run away from her family and return to him. It is she who takes the perilous journeys, climbing down from her tower, vaulting a wall and falling into a ditch, wandering through a forest beset with beasts and brambles; it is she who builds a house of lilies and grass for her lover in the woods, who leaves her newly-found family and country rather than be married to someone else, and who travels as a minstrel (normally a male role) singing of her love. Her behavior is sharply contrasted with that of the hero, who acts rather poorly throughout. He boasts about his love, clearly feeling it is superior to Nicolete's—he insists that women cannot love as well as men, that woman's love is in the eye, the nipple, the toe, while man's is planted in the heart (14, p. 18)—but his actions belie him. While she does everything possible to get to him, he feels sorry for himself, weeps a lot, lets himself be captured by his enemy because he is thinking about his love, and only begins to fight when he realizes that if his head is cut off he cannot speak to Nicolete (10). Later, thinking of her again, he trips on a stone in the woods and dislocates his shoulder. His loyalty to his love is intense, but it is entirely introverted and, far from inspiring him to great deeds, it has a negative effect. When his father renegs on his promise to let the lovers meet, Aucassin releases the enemy he has captured and enjoins him to make continual war on his father. When he is told he will go to hell if he perseveres in this love, he says he prefers hell, where he will find lovely knights and clerks and ladies who have had several lovers, to a heaven which is peopled by old priests and devout cripples (6).

We see an even more extreme reversal of roles in the kingdom of Torelore, where the king is in bed giving birth, and the queen out waging war with fruits and vegetables. Aucassin is disturbed by their behavior, though he seems to see nothing wrong in his own. He rips

---

et les ex vairs et rians et le face traitice et le nes haut et bien assis'' (12). *Aucassin et Nicolette,* ed. H. Suchier (1878; 8th ed. repr. New York; Stechert, 1936).

the bed clothes off the king and beats him, and he interferes in the
war, killing the enemy against the custom of the land. The idea of a
war in which no killing is permitted may simply be a fantastic detail
for the contemporary audience, but it is tantalizing to see in it some
hint that a world in which men have babies and women fight may in
some ways be better than the real world. The people of Torelore, in
any case, have no illusions about Aucassin—they want the king to
send him away and keep Nicolete for their son. Their customs may be
upside down, but they know true worth.

Aucassin et Nicolete is, of course, a parody romance in which
one expects exaggeration, but the reversal of sexual roles can be a factor in the conventional romance situation as well. Chrétien's Erec,
from the first, shows a tendency to ignore the realm of male activity
(the fellowship of Arthurian knights) for the queen's service. In the
first scene, he is riding unarmed, and is thus unable to defend the
queen's honor when it is attacked; after he marries Enide, he stays
alone with her and pays others to do his fighting for him. The an-
tisocial nature of his life is emphasized by his refusal to accept the
friendship of Guivret or the Arthurian court. He cuts himself off from
his society to devote himself entirely to his love, again essentially a
self-absorption, since Enide is an extension of Erec. But when she
voices some misgivings about his conduct he treats her as an alien figure; he forbids her to speak to him, and has her ride ahead of him as
the visible symbol of the inspiring lady. That is, as he has cut himself
off from society, he has in fact rejected a part of himself. It is clear
from the contests of the White-Stag and the Sparrow-Hawk at the
beginning of the romance that the union of man and woman symbolizes the union of prowess and beauty, and that the woman represents
the inspiration to action. In failing to act, Erec has denied Enide. He
does not want to acknowledge what she represents because that means
he must admit his own failure and so he forbids her to speak. However
she continues to warn him of danger in the first part of the journey, although he is by now alert to it himself. Language is a superfluous
means of communication between them. In fact, it is when she thinks

he cannot hear her that her sounds have their greatest effect—her laments when she thinks he is asleep, or her scream at the Count of Limors' attack when she thinks Erec is dead. Each time, she rouses him to a new awareness, first to the inadequacy of his life, then to the intensity of her loyalty. This proof of her devotion restores their understanding, and they ride off on the same horse, a symbol of their union. At the Joie de la Cort, Erec will understand Enide's thoughts without her speaking. His reunion with Enide signals his own perfection, which enables him to accept his proper role within society, first in the fellowship of Guivret and the Arthurian court, and then in the rule of his own land. The romance ends with the coronation of Erec and Enide, the ultimate symbol of personal integrity and public harmony.

By accepting his public responsibilities, Erec restores his identity as a man and as a knight and resolves the conflict within him which was symbolized by the rift with Enide. In *Le Chevalier de la Charette,* Chrétien again investigates the loss of identity of the knight in love who, in this case, surrenders his will completely to his lady. The conflict within the knight is externalized in the contrast between Lancelot and Gawain—Lancelot does what love demands, Gawain what reason dictates. That is, Lancelot takes the fastest if most dangerous road, and Gawain moves cautiously. It is true that, in the service of love, Lancelot achieves the great feat of rescuing the queen and Arthur's people from the kingdom of the dead, but he is also publicly disgraced at the tourney of Nouauz. When Guenievre functions as Lancelot's inspiration, she is a force for good, inspiring him to do what no other knight in his world can. But when he is in her presence, her effect is always destructive: when he looks down from a tower and sees her (the first time they come together in the romance) his instinct is to throw himself down; when he sees her at the window while he is fighting Meleagant, he turns to look at her instead of at his opponent; when she rejects him at Bademagu's court, he tries to commit suicide; and when he fights before her at the tourney of Nouauz, he makes a public fool of himself in order to please her. In other words, his image of her works well for him, but the reality of the woman works against him. The incongruity of the two is shown most forcefully in the tryst she grants him to make up for her abuse: when he comes to her he adores her, "an nul cors saint ne croit tant" (4653: he did not believe as fervently in any holy body),[17] and in the morning he kneels before her as if she were an altar (4718). But she is not a god or a saint, she is the wife of his king. By his blind devotion to her, he has in fact cut himself off from his lord. The tower in which Meleagant imprisons him (and where Chrétien leaves him when he stops writing) symbolizes Lancelot's situation—his love has cut him off completely from his world and from any opportunity to act effectively within it.

The symbolic function of the woman in this romance is complex because it must be seen in relation to two men, her husband, Arthur, and her lover, Lancelot. Arthur sacrifices her to preserve Kei, who represents the superficial honor of his court, thereby putting Guenievre in the hands of the thoroughly evil Meleagant. To preserve superficial honor, he allows the love that should inspire to right action to become the prisoner of lust and false honor. Only the pure devotion to love with no thought of worldly honor, which is embodied in Lancelot, can rescue the queen, but the one extreme countering the other does not restore the balance. The same tyranny Arthur exercises over Guenievre (she cannot refuse him when he sends her with Kei, although it endangers her life), she exercises over Lancelot, who cannot disobey her. So we have the abuse of love in marriage by the husband and the abuse of love-service by the lady. In this situation, it is not possible to achieve harmony within the individual or society. The Arthurian world itself is really the subject of this romance. Lancelot, Gawain, and Kei are all aspects of it and each of them shows up the limitations of its values. Kei is the selfish pursuit of honor for its own sake. Gawain is the reasonable pursuit of honor out of a higher sense of responsibility but, because he lacks the inspiration of love, he is no more successful than Kei. Lancelot, who has the proper motivation and succeeds in the deed, lacks the control of reason and therefore

[17] *Le Chevalier de la Charrete,* ed. M. Roques, *CFMA* (Paris: Champion, 1958).

fails in a deeper sense that is ultimately far more disruptive to his world.

In *Yvain,* the Arthurian world is still in a state of chaos, but Chrétien turns his attention to the individual. He embodies the hero's conflict in two ladies, a motif that occurs often in French romances of this period. In both *Yvain* and *Partenopeu de Blois,* the two women (one the love, the other a friend) represent the hero's heart and mind, or love and reason, and both serve the hero or are served by him in ways that are different but, finally, not incompatible. The second woman, the friend, helps the man with cleverness and control to win back the lady whom he had pursued with reckless passion and then lost by an equally reckless devotion to fighting. It is only through reason that he can achieve a proper balance of emotions. In the *Chevalier au Lion,* the conflict is not simply between love and reason, but between self-indulgence (the reckless pursuit of adventure and glory) and responsibility (controlled action in the service of others). The same wild impulse that leads Yvain to sneak out ahead of the court and pursue a wounded enemy into his castle also makes him fall violently in love with his victim's widow, his most obvious enemy, Laudine. At the same time, he is capable of reasonable, civilized behavior, as we learn from Lunette's allusion to their previous encounter. Throughout the romance he alternates between these two kinds of behavior, which are symbolized by his relations with the two women. With Laudine, he is either so passionately involved that he will risk death to be near her, or he forgets her and his responsibility to her land altogether while he is pursuing meaningless adventures with Gawain. Laudine represents the impulse to action, the uncontrolled desire for love or glory. His reconciliation with her, like his marriage, is arranged by Lunette's cleverness. Lunette to whom Yvain is attached by an increasingly complicated series of mutual obligations, represents rational control over action. It is she who protects him from his enemies when he is Laudine's captive, and who wins his lady for him, while he who had helped her in the past rescues her from death when her own lover, Gawain, cannot. Chrétien is making a double point with their relationship: first, that friendship is a far more reliable kind of commitment than romantic love and, secondly, that it is only when action is carried out under the control of reason that it is valid.

In the first part of the romance Yvain's adventures, like his falling in love, are reckless and, as far as we know, pointless. His pursuit of glory makes him forget his love—one passion conflicts with the other and the result is that the hero loses his mind. The adventures that follow his recovery are all for carefully defined purposes—to rescue victims of others' passions, violence or lust—and they are arranged on a rigid time schedule, a detail which further emphasizes the importance of self-control. But Yvain can only be restored to harmony in his passions (symbolized by the reconciliation with Laudine) through the offices of Lunette, his reason. His union with Laudine combines love and glory since he won her, in a sense, by fighting, and his marriage involves him in continual fighting to defend her fountain. Yvain needs both women, and both have something to give him: Laudine's love is symbolized by the ring that protects him from harm; Lunette's help is symbolized by the ring that makes him invisible to his enemies. However pessimistic the end of Yvain may be in terms of social service,[18] in private terms at least the hero does achieve the reintegration of his personality.

Partenopeu de Blois presents a situation that recalls *Yvain* in many ways. It portrays a lady who does not interfere with the hero's duties to family and country (though they endanger his commitment to her), but who is adamant in her rejection when he fails her, and who must be tricked into reconciliation by another woman, in this case her sister, who manipulates both lovers to their advantage. However, the emphasis in this romance is not on the proper purpose of action but on the demands of love—on the need to ignore worldly pressures and accept the responsibilities of love—and this is a lesson that must be learnt by the woman as well as the man. Both of them find it difficult

---

[18] I have discussed that aspect of *Yvain* and what seems to me to be a progressive disillusionment with chivalry on Chrétien's part in "The Conflict of Lyric Conventions and Romance Form," *In Pursuit of Perfection.*

to deny the conventions of their societies, however superficial, and each therefore endangers the love. His society particularly is based on false values and employs deception and intrigue to interfere with love.

The heroine, Melior, chooses Partenopeu as the most promising young knight she can find (he is thirteen at the time), draws him to her by magic, and keeps him with her secretly until he is old enough to be presented to her people. In public she attempts to preserve the appearance of indifference to love, while in private she indulges her desires. She pretends to fear the popular reaction to her lover, although his reputation and lineage were good enough to attract her. She insists on maintaining conventions when they make little sense: though she has got him there by magic she pretends to be surprised to find him in her bed and repulses his first tentative moves in order to make him appear the aggressor; and at the end of the romance, she feigns preference for someone else in order to hide her feelings for him. Partenopeu makes the same kind of error when he leaves her to return to his land and serve his people: though at first impervious to the machinations of his mother and his king, Partenopeu does eventually succumb to the seduction of the bishop ("tant l'a par losenge encanté," 4439).[19] Neither the bishop nor his mother can see beyond the magic powers of the lady he loves, so they suspect her of devilry. Ironically, it was love that awakened him to a sense of responsibility for his own people, and love that increased his ability to serve them.

Partenopeu's people do not understand the nature of Melior's love, but he has known the fruits of that love—the joy and understanding and generosity—and should not have been swayed. All that had been denied him was what the world sees, the surface appearance of the lady (who came to him only in the dark). When he insists on seeing her with the world's eyes, using his mother's lantern to look at her, he loses her. The lady has a similar problem of vision. She has kept him invisible to her people, just as she has kept herself invisible to him, using magic, in contrast to Laudine, to protect herself more

[19] *Partenopeu de Blois, A French Romance of the Twelfth Century,* ed. J. Gildea, 3 vol. (Villanova University Press, 1967, 1968, 1970).

than her lover. She is afraid to let Partenopeu be seen because apparently, despite her love for him, she does not properly appreciate him. When he returns to her tourney at the end of the romance she herself cannot see him clearly, first because he is in disguise, and then because his combat moves into a tower. In a clear reversal of the earlier scene with his mother's lantern, she comes to the tower with lights, discovers that it is really he, and is unable to embrace him because others are present. Both lovers are misled, by a concern with surface appearance, to see with the world's eyes rather than with the deeper vision of love.

There are obvious Cupid-Psyche analogies in this romance, but the roles are reversed. Psyche's part is taken by the man, and the god of love is played by the woman. The force of love, once again, operates through the woman: she draws the man to her by magic, and she creates new worlds for both of them to share (she can make thousands of knights appear and disappear at her pleasure.)[20] The exercise of reason, as in *Yvain,* operates through a second woman, Melior's sister, Uraque. She travels back and forth between her sister and the hero, forcing both of them, step by step, towards a recognition of their errors and a reconciliation. She makes Melior see the unfairness of her behavior towards Partenopeu and, more important, she makes her see that, despite her learning and her arts, she is also vulnerable to love and must suffer for her unwillingness to admit it. Uraque also prepares Partenopeu—by rescuing him from danger, by restoring him to health, and by feeding his courage with hope based on false messages from Melior. What the author is saying, through Uraque, is that for man and woman both it is not enough to love; one must be aware of the true nature of love and fully accept the responsibilities it brings.

At the same time, the author's concern with the heroine's atti-

---

[20] Her level of education is striking: she was taught the seven arts, medicine, theology, necromancy, and enchantment (4573 ff); cf. Isolt, who is educated only in literature and music, but to a similarly high level. In both cases, however, the women are connected with magic, Isolt through her mother, Melior in her own practice, suggesting that too much education in women is dangerous.

tude towards love is to some extent occasioned by his own love, which he gives as his reason for writing the romance. Every lover, he admits, thinks his lady is the best, "la millor" (9229–30), which is just as well or everyone would be in love with my lady who is without equal. Since the heroine's name, Melior, is a form of "the best," the poet is making a connection between her and his own lady. In the days of romance, the poet complains, men were able to conquer ladies by means of their beauty, chivalry, and courtesy, but now women go to church and lead chaste lives—they are "deaf with chastity" (8086: *sordes sunt de chastée*). His own lady hides herself from him, though, unlike his hero, he would never betray her. Through Melior, in other words, the poet criticizes his lady for refusing to admit her love and, presumably, for refusing to give it.

The author of *Li Biaus Desconneus* also uses his romance to make a point with his lady. He presents his hero with a choice between two ladies, the one he prefers but leaves, and the other, who plots to get him and succeeds. The poet uses the hero's predicament as a kind of blackmail to his own lady, saying that he will only allow the hero to return to his true love if the poet's lady will be kind to him.[21] The hero's choice between the two ladies is thus at least partly a ploy to serve the poet's private purpose; nonetheless a real conflict is involved, one that can be found in several other romances. The problem of two women also faces the hero in *Horn,* where he chooses love, and again in *Ille et Galeron,* in *Eliduc,* and in *Tristan,* where the hero commits himself to the other woman because he is unsure of himself or of his love. One lady is the hero's first love and represents all that love can offer—a new identity, the inspiration to great deeds, his highest aspirations—but her service demands devotion and sacrifice, sometimes even worldly disgrace. The other lady is part of the con-

---

[21] Haidu suggests that the three ladies represent a choice among genres and the different kinds of love described in them: the fairy illustrates love from the lai tradition; the courtly lady, from romance; and the poet's lady, from the lyric. P. Haidu, "Realism, Convention, Fictionality and the Theory of Genres in *Le Bel Inconnu," L'Esprit Créateur,* 12 (1972) 37–60.

ventional world, to be won and served without difficulty by the normal exercise of chivalry; she offers wealth, high position, marriage, but not love, at least not the love he wants. The second is a pale reflection of the first; she represents what is actually possible in this life, or the reality that underlies the magic of love after it has lost its power. The choice the hero makes, sometimes against his will, depends on his attachment to worldly values or on his sense of his own value, of his ability to be worthy of his love. That the choice arises at all indicates that a conflict already exists in the hero, that he is not at peace with himself.

In *Li Biaus Desconneu,* the hero's love is never named; she is simply called "la Pucele." She draws him to her from afar as Melior did in *Partenopeu,* though not by magic; she sends Hélie to fetch him. In some ways, Hélie resembles the Lunette-Uraque lady, personifying reason and serving as the knight's guide, for she reminds him continually of his commitment and finds ways to rescue him from circumstances that threaten to hinder him. It is significant that Hélie is a servant of the lady who is Love (not the lady who is connected with chivalry and the Arthurian world), but the adventure she leads him to is the rescue of the other lady. That is one of the trials that prove him a worthy knight, but it also involves him with a woman who will conspire to take him away from his love. The lady who is Love gives the hero his identity literally as well as symbolically—she tells him he is Guinglain, Gawain's son—as she has given him the opportunity to win glory through adventure. To some extent, she is also trapped by the conventions of the chivalric world: in a situation that recalls the Joie de la Cort in Chrétien's *Erec,* she dwells in a castle with a knight who fights all comers and puts their heads on stakes around the wall; if he is victorious for seven years he will marry her, although she does not want him. (It is tempting, but probably wrong, to see in this situation a perspective on adventure from the woman's point of view.) By defeating this knight, Guinglain frees the lady, giving her the opportunity to exercise her choice just as her love has enabled him to act. He passes all her trials, both as knight and lover. When he tries to make his way to her at night, uncertain whether she meant him to come, he encounters nightmarish dangers which terrify him but which disappear when he calls for help, leaving him exposed to ridicule. Presumably these trials are meant to show that, having won glory as a knight, he must undergo shame as well to be worthy of love. On the other hand, they also suggest either that much of the magic of love is in his mind, or that whereas he can meet the dangers of chivalry without fear, love asks too much of him. The force of love which inspires and rules, which gives courage and glory and joy, demands a more perfect devotion. In any case, chivalry wins out and the hero deserts his love. Her magic has controlled his destiny until the love is consummated, but then, having given him his identity and his position in the world, it releases him, leaving him free to accept its gifts or return to his world. He chooses the world, leaving his love to go to a tourney that was planned by the other lady to lure him away, knowing he will not be able to return. What this lady offers is the conventional reward of a wife and a kingdom—not to be scorned, but lacking the fulfillment of love.

Generally, when the man becomes involved with a second woman, it is due to some inadequacy or doubt in him, which leaves him vulnerable to her advances, as if by his doubts he denied the existence of the first or at least his right to her. This is less true of Horn than of the other heroes mentioned above, but even Horn refuses the heroine's offer of love because he feels unworthy and must prove himself first. "You can't promise yourself to me," he tells Rigmel, "you could marry the son of an emperor" (1262–63).[22] When he finally does excel in battle and can accept her ring, he is slandered by an envious companion and must leave. In his travels, he becomes involved with another girl; he serves her family and is offered the girl and the land in reward. (Cf. *Tristan,* where the hero encounters an almost identical situation with the second Isolt.) But Horn returns to his love, rescues her from an unwanted marriage and marries her. Thus he

[22] *The Romance of Horn* by Thomas, ed. M. K. Pope, Anglo-Norman Texts (Oxford: Blackwell, 1955).

follows the pattern of romance love to its simplest conclusion: he has received his first impetus to action from his love, has proven himself worthy of her, and now takes a new identity from her, remaining to rule in her land, not his own. The second lady, Lenburc, is more accessible than the first—he won her quickly with the consent of her family—but she cannot replace Rigmel. The distance between the two women is revealed in Lenburc's attempt to sing a lay about Rigmel, which she cannot even finish. Horn disposes of his obligation to Lenburc by marrying her to his cousin, perhaps a pale reflection of him as Lenburc is of Rigmel.

Horn's doubts of himself or his lady's love are minimal and his involvement with Lenburc, though momentarily embarrassing, does not go far, so it is fairly easy for him to discharge that responsibility and return to his love. It is not usually so easy to resolve the problem. In *Ille et Galeron,* Gautier d'Arras presents a more complicated version of a similar triangle. His hero cannot resolve his doubts before he marries and so he has no confidence in his wife's love for him. Although he is a successful fighter, and acceptable to the lady's brother, he does not feel he has proved himself. It is she who obtains her brother's permission to marry him, since the hero does not dare ask. When, after their marriage, he loses an eye in a tourney, he is sure he will lose her too. This is a failure of inner vision, symbolized by the loss of the eye—an inability to grasp the true extent of her love, which he sees only from the world's limited view. He is unsure of her love for him because he is unsure of his right to that love. So he leaves his wife, but by the time he has achieved enough worldly success to feel worthy of her, he has become involved with a second woman, Ganor. He has, following the conventional pattern of the second woman, defended her father's land and won the daughter and half the country. However, he is still in love with his wife, Galeron, whom he fortunately meets before he can marry Ganor. He is able to accept his wife's love now because their worldly positions are reversed: she has spent all her resources in the search for him. Nonetheless, the resolution is not entirely satisfactory, for in achieving his new position he

has had to commit himself to Ganor. He spends the rest of the romance torn between his love for Galeron and his compassion for
Ganor, the penalty of his failure to trust his wife's love in the first
place. Eventually his wife becomes a nun and Ille, with great hesita-
tion and much prodding, marries Ganor. One is left with the strong
sense that the second lady never replaces the first and that it was only
because he had failed the first that he had to accept the second.[23]

   Eliduc, in Marie de France's lai, involves himself similarly
with a second woman through a failure of loyalty to his wife, and
finds himself at the center of a painful triangle.[24] He appears to be an
innocent victim of fate at the beginning of the lai, a good husband and
vassal who falls into disfavor with his king for no apparent reason. But
when he goes into exile, though he does his best to serve his host, he
is again met by doubts. One begins to sense that there is a weakness in
him, which emerges in his relations with the girl who falls in love with
him in the new land. He indulges himself with her, accepting her gifts
and attention and doing nothing to discourage her feeling, despite his
pledge of loyalty to his wife. When he is summoned home by his king,
he realizes that he has acted badly, but he still fails to admit that
he is married and thus to end the new relationship. Instead he leaves,
only to return shortly and take the girl away with him. When she acci-
dentally learns the truth, it almost kills her. It is Eliduc's wife, whose
devotion and generosity never flag, who nurses her back to health and
then takes herself out of the way by retiring to a convent. In this case,
one feels that the hero has lost the better woman because he was unworthy of her. Eventually, he and his new wife follow her example,

[23] Fourrier says of Ille's feeling for Ganor: "l'unité de caractère n'est pas rompue, et
l'auteur a réussi ce tour de force de faire nâitre l'amour du héros pour Ganor de son
amour pour Galeron" [*Le Courant Réaliste dans le Roman courtois en France au
Moyen Age,* Vol. 1, *Les Débuts* (Paris: Nizet, 1960), p. 297], which is true but fails, I
think, to take into account the painfulness of his resignation to the second marriage.

[24] Because I am following themes, rather than a chronological development, I have
taken *Ille* before *Eliduc,* on which it was apparently based. For a discussion of Gautier's
use of Marie, see P. Nykrog, "Two Creators of Narrative Form in Twelfth Century
France: Gautier d'Arras—Chrétien de Troyes," *Speculum* 48 (1973), 258–76.

and give up the world themselves, which is perhaps the only satisfactory solution.

The Tristan story, as Thomas tells it, presents the most interesting statement on a psychological level of the conflict embodied in two women, but it also introduces the problem of adultery. In the other romances we have discussed (with the exception of *Lancelot,* where the fact of adultery is not really faced), the hero's love was free to give herself to him if he chose her. But in *Tristan,* she is married and her husband is the hero's uncle and king. In order to choose love, in this case, the hero must betray his lord. It is interesting that in romance when a man is torn between two women, he does not normally commit adultery—a way may even be found for him to marry both (as in *Ille et Galeron, Eliduc*). But when a woman is caught between two men, she betrays her husband and her marriage vows and involves her lover in a conflict of loyalty. It is true that in *Tristan* the hero also marries, so that technically he too commits adultery when he returns to the queen, but only Isolt's adultery is treated as such in the story. In cases where the man is caught between two women, the women represent different aspects of his aspirations; but when the woman is caught between two men, she represents a destructive passion. From society's point of view, of course, adultery is dangerous, both spiritually and politically. It is not surprising, then, that adulterous heroines, even if their behavior is partially excused by the pettiness of their husbands (as in *Eracle*), are rarely presented as inspirations to good. Only Marie de France, who sees marriage from the woman's point of view as repressive and even sinful, allows the adulterous wife a noble love.

In Thomas' *Tristan,* the adultery is really an accident of fate, since the seeds of love were planted before Isolt's marriage to Mark. But the adulterous nature of their relationship becomes central to the plot and it exacerbates Tristan's inner conflict. It is his jealousy of Isolt, his curiosity about her relations with her husband, that lead him into flirtation and marriage with Isolt-as-blanschemains, a marriage which does not solve his problem, but only extends the circle of those who suffer from love. Love means suffering for everyone who experiences it, Thomas tells us: *Qui unc ne sot que est dolur/ ne pot saver que est amur* (Douce, 991–92: who has never known what pain is, cannot know what love is). But in Tristan it is his heritage from his mother, for whom love was a poison, a disease, and death.[25]

The woman Tristan loves incarnates the destructive force of love, the all-consuming passion that excludes any other ties. She unleashes the destructive impulse in him, the death-wish, bringing on the surrender of a noble spirit to a passion that must kill him. (She dominates the action in Thomas' version more than in any other.) In a way, she draws him to her by magic (the poison on Morolt's sword comes from her mother); she gives him new life (her mother cures him of that wound and later of the dragon's poison); and she awakens him to the passion of love (the love-potion, too, comes from her mother). She is unswerving in her devotion to him, but she is possessive: if she must die, she wants him to die too, so he cannot love anyone else (Douce, 1615 ff). Her character is passionate and violent: when she learns that Tristan is the man who killed her uncle, she rushes to attack him and is stopped only by her hatred for the steward, which is stronger than her desire for revenge. She is suspicious of Brangene and tries to have her murdered, and when that fails she turns on the murderers. Her love does not inspire the hero to action; on the contrary, it is the wounds he incurs in fighting that make him vulnerable to love. Love isolates him from his world, not in joy but in pain.[26]

It is because of his innate tendency toward suffering that Tris-

[25] *Les Fragments du Roman de Tristan,* ed. B. H. Wind (Genève: Droz, 1960). Details of the story that are not found in the Thomas fragments are taken from the Scandinavian translation of Brother Robert. For a detailed treatment on the differences between the major versions, see Ferrante, *The Conflict of Love and Honor* (The Hague: Mouton, 1973).

[26] Gottfried tells virtually the same story, but changes the emphasis altogether; for his hero, love is an exaltation, born of higher sensibilities, that enables him to reach heights of ecstasy unknown to others. It is a shared love, whose finest moment comes in the *Minnegrotte* when Tristan and Isolt are alone together, but it is a love that the world cannot contain. It exists in its perfection only in their minds.

tan's attempts to alleviate it by seeking the company of the other Isolt do not succeed either. She is a reflection of Isolt the queen in many ways: she has the same name and the same artistic gifts, though to a lesser degree; she is suspicious and, like the queen, she eavesdrops on her husband; and when she feels herself betrayed she does not hesitate to take revenge. The fact that she has the heroine's name suggests that the hero's love is his own creation, and that for him women are differentiated only by the degree to which they reflect his image. All the major women in the story share the negative traits—Brangene can be unscrupulous in her devotion (giving what remains of the potion to Mark to bind him to a woman who can never love him), and she can be violent and vindictive when she feels abused. The only figure from which Tristan can derive satisfaction without danger or pain is the statue he has had made of Isolt, the image he created of his love as he wanted her to be, existing entirely through and for him.

Gautier, also, reveals a negative view of women and love in *Eracle,* but he shows even more strongly than Thomas that the defect in love lies in the man. Though this romance is a tale of adultery, Gautier shifts the emphasis to the husband rather than to the lover, and keeps his hero free of love involvements altogether. In fact, Eracle, the emperor's counselor, is the voice of reason, which the emperor does not always heed. When the emperor decides to marry, Eracle finds him the one virtuous woman in his realm. Not satisfied with the ideal woman, who in this case actually exists, the husband turns her into a normal, i.e. sinful, woman by imposing on her his own idea of woman. Instead of relying on her demonstrated virtue, as Eracle tries to persuade him to do, he locks her up when he goes off to war. She, not unnaturally, is offended by this unjust punishment and does what he is afraid she will do, and what most characters in the story expect women to do—she takes a lover. When her affair is discovered she goes off with her lover, leaving the emperor alone with the fate he has chosen for himself. This is a reversal of the pattern of the man embodying his ideal in the woman only to discover that the ideal never existed. In this case he embodies a lesser vision in her, only to discover that the ideal did exist and that he has destroyed it. It is, of course, his love that is defective; incapable of perfect faith himself, he cannot believe it exists in another and so he loses it.

In all the romances so far discussed in this chapter, the woman has embodied the force of love that works in the man, for good or ill; she is a projection of the man's image or desires. Occasionally, she is presented as a victim of the social conventions of chivalry or marriage, but always the focus has been on the man's psychology. In the laies of Marie de France, however, we are shown love as a facet of female psychology as well, and we see, in *Yonec*, that the man can be a projection of the woman's mind. A possessive old man has married a young wife on the pretence of wanting children, but they have had none, presumably because such self-indulgence is sterile. He keeps her locked up in a tower, not even allowing her to leave to go to church. She turns her mind to chivalric adventures of knights and ladies, of love without blame. She creates a love in her mind, wills it, and it comes to her in the shape of a great bird which turns into a handsome knight under her gaze. His existence depends on her desire: he could not have come, he tells her, until she asked; and to prove that he is not from the devil he takes her form to receive the eucharist, i.e., he is a reflection of her image. He will come whenever she wants him, but if anyone suspects his existence he will die. Unfortunately, she cannot conceal the change that love works in her and her husband becomes suspicious; though he cannot see the lover, he knows there is something because she is happy. He lays a trap for the bird and wounds it; once the outer world intrudes on her fantasy, the vision is spoiled. Now the love becomes a dream: the lady leaps from the tower in which she has been imprisoned [27] and follows the dying bird to a city of

[27] No prison can contain love in Marie, because love is in the mind, cf. *Guigemar,* below, pp. 96–97. This motif also occurs in Chrétien: the wall of air around the Joie de la Cort in *Erec* holds the lovers in because they will their captivity; the secret garden where the lovers hide in *Cliges* seems impenetrable, but is easily scaled by Bertran; Lancelot is immured in a tower, but leaves it without difficulty to attend a tourney at which the queen will be present.

silver where everyone is asleep. He gives her a ring to make her husband forget, and a sword for her son, and somehow she returns to her tower; but for the son, it is as if the love had never been. That son, more the child of her heart than her body, will eventually kill her husband to avenge his father. The love that came to fill her need, gives her the means and the will to escape her prison and finally to destroy her captor. If we are to take the lover as a real being, then their love is fruitful while the marriage was sterile; if, as seems more likely, the whole story is her fantasy, then it is through her child that the woman gives reality to her love, and it is the love that endures.

The power of love to free the soul from the constraints of the world can work for a man as well, as Marie shows in *Lanval*. Lanval is undeservedly neglected at Arthur's court when honors are distributed, although he is known for his valor and generosity. Only love gives him what the world denies and protects him when the world turns against him. A fairy rescues him from his unhappiness, offering rich gifts and love, and promising to come whenever he wants her as long as he keeps her existence a secret. Like the wife in *Yonec* he is now happy in his isolation, but the world does not leave him to enjoy it—as if the joy of love compelled a confrontation with the world. The queen, perhaps sensing something special in him now as the old husband did in *Yonec,* makes advances to him; in the course of the ensuing quarrel he boasts about his love, thus betraying his promise. Nonetheless, when he is brought to trial to answer the queen's false accusations, love forgives him, although he has wronged her, while the court condemns him for something he has not done. When the lady comes to court to vindicate him, he does not hesitate to make his choice: he leaps on her horse and rides off with her to Avalun, for none of the world's treasures can equal love's.

In *Guigemar,* neither the hero nor the heroine has known love. The hero, suffering from a wound that can only be healed by a woman who will endure hardship for his love, is carried by a strange ship to a tower in which a young queen is imprisoned by her old and jealous husband. She lives surrounded by images of love—her chamber is decorated with paintings of Venus and of love-service—but without love. The love that develops between her and the hero is expressed and bestowed without hypocrisy or false modesty. It is symbolized by the knots they exchange, which only they can undo. This is a protection that works, unlike the towers of jealous husbands, because it is love that binds them and they freely accept that bond. When the husband eventually discovers them, the boat appears to take them away, first the lover and two years later the lady. Once again, love provides both the will and the means to escape the restraints or dangers of the world. Before they are reunited, the woman falls into the hands of another man who cannot undo the knot, but refuses to give her up, forcing Guigemar to kill him. The men that would hold her captive or possess her against her will seem to be interchangeable, while the only power that can really hold her is the love she has freely chosen.

The ease with which physical obstacles are surmounted in Marie's stories is less a facet of the fantastic than an indication of her psychology of love. Love exists in the mind, which is free to act as it will. The world may control the body, but only temporarily, only until the mind asserts itself, until the individual finds his will through love. Then nothing can hinder him or her. The power that Marie attributes to love is not very different from many of the romances we have looked at, but for her it is more than a force that inspires the lover and gives him a new sense of himself; it is also a means of overcoming the pains of the world. It frees the lover's imagination from the bonds that society imposes on it, and it is a gift that women can partake of as fully as men.

Chapter Four

In the
Thirteenth Century

There is a sharp contrast between the works we have so far considered and the major works of the thirteenth century in their presentation of women. The concept of woman as a part of man—of the union of man and woman as a symbol of the harmony and integration of the man's being—no longer has much force. The possibility of harmony, either of a man within himself or of the individual in society, seems remote. The atmosphere in literature is one of fear and danger, of discord and fragmentation. In the external world of Arthurian romance, the fellowship of knights disintegrates, individuals seek the salvation of their own souls rather than the defence of others; in the internal world of the soul, the separate parts work against each other, unable to find a uniting force (as in the *Roman de la Rose* and lyric poetry). A substitute for harmony is sought, perhaps, in the compilations, the vast encyclopedias and Summas in which everything is discussed and categorized but not really integrated, or in the romance cycles, in which all the stories are put together, but the world that holds them falls apart. Literary attention focuses more and more on the individual and less on his relation to society, because it is only by cutting himself off from the world around him that man can be saved. Personal salvation is achieved at the cost of social dissolution.

In this atmosphere, woman is no longer presented as a part of man, a part that is lower but still essential to his perfection. She is a separate being who, for the most part, endangers his soul because she provides him the opportunity to indulge his lower impulses. She must be avoided or rejected, not assimilated. Woman is now seen solely in terms of her physical function; she is tolerated as a necessary evil to bear children and maintain the species. Only mystics and lyric poets still attribute any positive powers to women (and it is a combination of these two strains that emerges in Dante's *Comedy*). Even lyric poets, however, though they preserve the convention of woman as a beneficial influence, see her as an instrument rather than a force in herself. They speak of women as superhuman beings, heavenly creatures endowed by God with special powers to move men, but primarily a medium through which God's influence can work. Instead of becoming independent figures, they have become tools of higher (or lower) forces, alien even to the men who write about them. No longer symbols of male qualities or projections of male ideals, they become vessels to serve man's needs, either carrying his children or relaying God's grace. The ideal thirteenth century woman is the Virgin Mary, who is both chaste child-bearer and intercessor, the mediator through whom God reaches man and man reaches God. She is man's defense against sin; indeed, Bonaventure claims that man cannot reach God except through her. Thus she has a real power that women in twelfth-century literature possessed only symbolically. But as a real woman she is unique, hence even further removed from womankind than the personifications and symbols of the earlier period.

In this chapter, the individual genres will not be covered as extensively as they were for the twelfth century. Only a few major works or writers from each area will be discussed: Thomas Aquinas and Bonaventure (religious interpretation); the *Roman de la Rose* (allegory); the Arthurian vulgate cycle (romance); and the Italian poets of the *dolce stil nuovo* (lyric).[1] In the thirteenth century, the interest in biblical exegesis is not as strong as it had been, not at least among the first rank of theologians. Beryl Smalley offers many reasons for this: the Aristotelian aversion to seeking hidden meanings not expressed by the text, the intellectual interest in theological questions rather than in-

---

[1] Bonaventure, Thomas Aquinas, and the dolce stilnovisti were chosen not only for their intrinsic importance, but also because of their influence on Dante.

terpretation, the mystical discouragement of reading, and the decline in humanist culture which the twelfth century had developed but the thirteenth neglected in favor of science and metaphysics.[2] To get a sense of Aquinas and Bonaventure on women, then, we must look at their major works as well as their exegesis.[3]

Aquinas is conventional in his views of women, along the lines traced in early exegesis and the *Glossa Ordinaria,* but he is, if anything, more negative, drawing heavily on Paul and Aristotle, "the Apostle" and "the Philosopher." Both Paul and Aristotle play down the role of women, Paul saying that they should not preach, Aristotle that they are unfit to govern and, most damaging of all, that they are defects of nature. The idea of woman as *mas* or *masculus occasionatus,* a male manqué, is quoted frequently by Aquinas [4] and seems to underlie many of his attitudes. He considers women to be weaker and more inclined to sin than men, both in nature and in body: their humors are more abundant, therefore they are more easily overcome by concupiscence (*ST,* Suppl., q. 62, a. 4); they are softer in body, therefore more given to sin; and they are weaker in reason, therefore less able to resist sin (*1 Tim.,* ch. V, lect. i and *ST* 2-2, q. 156, a. 1 and q. 149, a. 4). They like to adorn themselves outside because they lack

[2] *The Study of the Bible in the Middle Ages* (1952; repr. University of Notre Dame Press, 1964); see particularly pp. 281, 283, 293, and 329.

[3] The works of Thomas Aquinas that were consulted for this chapter are the *Summa Theologica, Catena aurea in quattuor Evangelia, Expositio in omnes S. Pauli Epistolas,* and commentaries on the Gospels of Matthew and John, and on the Sentences of Peter Lombard. The edition used is Sancti Thomae Aquinatis Doctoris Angelici Ordinis Praedicatorum *Opera Omnia* (1852–73; repr. New York: Musurgia Pub., 1949), Vol. I–IV, VI–VIII and X–XIII. For the *Summa,* the Eng. trans. of the Fathers of the English Dominican Province, 3 vol. (New York: Benziger, 1947, 1948), was consulted. Bonaventure's works included the *Collationes in Hexaemeron, In quattuor libros Senteniarum Expositio, Itinerarium Mentis in Deum, Breviloquim, Collationes,* and several short mystical pieces. The edition used is SRE Cardinalis S. Bonaventurae, *Opera Omnia,* ed. A. C. Peltier (Paris: Vives, 1865), Vol. I–V, VIII, and IX. An English translation, *The Works of Bonaventure,* trans. J. de Vinck, 5 vol. (Paterson: St. Anthony Guild, 1960–69), was also consulted.

[4] See *1 Cor.,* ch. XI, lectio I; *ST* 1, q. 92, a. 1, and q. 99, a. 2; *ST* 2-1, q. 102, a. 3.

inner, spiritual beauty, and they lack inner beauty because that comes only when all things are ordered and disposed by reason, in which women are defective (1 *Tim.*, ch. II, lect. ii).[5] The sexual characteristics that distinguish women are all interpreted as signs of sin: the impurity of woman suffering from the monthly flow of blood denotes either the impurity of idolatry, because of the blood-offering, or the impurity of mind sensualized by pleasure; the impurity of sexual intercourse and of woman in childbirth signifies the impurity of original sin (*ST* 2-1, q. 102, a. 5).

Commenting on the genealogy of Christ that is given in the gospel of Matthew, Thomas notes that the only women mentioned are sinners in order to show that Christ came to redeem sinners (Mt. 1). It is their sex that makes women sinful, hence subject to men, and that prevents them from performing certain social functions: they cannot teach, as Paul ordered, because a teacher is a *pre*late or *pre*sider; a woman cannot *pre*cede, she can only follow, since she is defective in reason, which is essential to leadership (1 *Cor.*, ch. XIV, lect. vii).[6] On the other hand, men who are subject may teach because they are subject not by their nature, as women are, but by accident (*ST* 2-2, q. 177, a. 2). Woman does not differ from man as to *res,* what she is (a human being, body and soul), but as to *signum,* what she represents. Since priesthood is a sacrament, a *signum* as well as *res,* the female, in a state of subjection, cannot signify the eminence of degree that a

[5] "Sicut mulieres sunt mollioris corporis quam viri, ita et debilioris rationis. Rationis autem est ordinare actus et effectus uniuscujusque rei. Ornatus vero consistit in debita ordinatione et dispositione. Sic in interiori decore nisi sint omnia ordinata ex dispositione per rationem non habent pulchritudinem spiritualem. Et ideo, quia mulieres deficiunt a ratione, requirit ab eis ornatum." Cf. 1 Cor., ch. XI, lect. ii: "a man ought not cover his head, it is not natural for him, but for a woman it is; women have a natural disposition and interior inclination. . . . It is more suitable to the condition of women to use an artificial covering of the head."

[6] This is a loose translation of the Latin in order to preserve the play on the prefix: "Unde cum docere dicat *prae*lationem et *prae*sidentiam, non decet eas quae subditae sunt. Ratio autem quae subditae sunt, et non *prae*sunt, est quia deficiunt ratione, quae est maxime necessaria *prae*sidenti."

priest represents (*ST,* Suppl., q. 39, a. 1). Thomas is careful to distinguish prophecy from teaching, since there are women prophets in the Old Testament. Prophecy is different, he explains, because God enlightens the mind so the natural disposition is irrelevant. That is, God does the work; the mind of the prophet need only receive, not think. Thomas does note that women were capable of great love for God, (Mt. 27), even that they were the first to see Him rise in glory because their love was more persistent (*ST,* 3, q. 55, a. 1),[7] but he is scornful of the value of their testimony. He tells us that Paul does not speak of Christ's appearances to women which had been related in the gospels, but refers instead to His appearances to men, even those not mentioned in the gospels. He did so because he was attempting to confute the infidels and therefore had to use "only authentic testimony," i.e., the testimony of men not validated by the evangelists is better than the authenticated testimony of women (1 *Cor.,* ch. XV, lect. i).[8] Even the Virgin Mary is put down, albeit gently. She no doubt received the gifts of wisdom, miracles, and prophecy in high degree, Thomas concedes, but not in order to *use* them—not to teach, but to contemplate, as befitted her condition of life, i.e., her sex (*ST* 3, q. 27, a. 5). Her marriage to Joseph was necessary partly so that Christ's genealogy could be traced back through a man (*ST* 3, q. 28, a. 1); Joseph had to be of the same tribe so it would be the true genealogy.

It is ironic that on the rare occasion when Thomas attributes positive symbolism to a female figure he uses it to justify the subjection of women. Following an unusual tradition, he says the bride of Canticles signifies Christ, the groom the Church militant, in which there are many corruptions; hence, for marriage, a husband is required only not to have been married, a wife is required both not to have been

---

[7] In the same passage, however, he notes that woman was the first to announce the resurrection as she was the first to bring death to man (cf. *Gloss*).

[8] "Et horum ratio fuit, quia Apostolus vult ex ratione confutare infideles et ideo noluit ponere testimonia nisi authentica; et ideo tacuit apparitiones mulieribus factas, et posuit quasdam quae non inveniuntur, ut ostendat, quod etiam aliis pluribus apparuit."

married *and* to be a virgin, like Christ (*ST,* Suppl., q. 66, a. 3).[9]
Thomas has many interesting things to say about marriage, several of
which reveal the deep anti-feminism we have noted. In the very word,
matrimony, are the roots of mother and matter, he points out, because
woman's only purpose is to bear children; therefore, she has a closer
relation to the nature of marriage than man, who was created for other
purposes (*ST,* Suppl., q. 44, a. 2). The male unites with the female
only to reproduce. In other activities he acts apart from her, since male
activities are nobler. Indeed, for all acts but generation, man would
have been better off with another man as his helpmate (*ST* 1,
q. 92, a. 1).[10]

But although marriage is the woman's realm, she is not to
dominate within it or within the family. The father should be loved
more than the mother because he is the principle of origin in a more
excellent way, the active principle (*ST* 2-2, q. 26, a. 10). In matters
that may affect the good of the offspring, the woman must be bound
by the needs of the unbegotten child, the man can indulge his desires.
A man may divorce his leprous wife for the sake of his progeny (*ST,*
Suppl., q. 67, a. 6), but a woman is bound to have sexual intercourse
with a leprous husband if he demands it, even though the child thus
begotten may be diseased, for it is better to be born diseased than not
to live at all (*ST,* Suppl., q. 64, a. 1).[11] Similarly, a man should not
lie with his wife when she is menstruating because it might harm the
child, but if he asks her she cannot refuse him; she, however, cannot

[9] He uses the more traditional interpretation, equating the bride with the church and the
groom with Christ, in connection with Paul's command that husbands love their wives
as Christ loved the Church, by which Paul meant the husband is the head of the wife as
Christ is of the church.

[10] M. Müller, *Die Lehre des Heiligen Augustinus von der Paradiesehe,* p. 262, says that
the great difference between the attitudes of Thomas and Hugo of St. Victor on marriage
is that Thomas works from animals to men, then turns his eye to God, while Hugo
works out from God and sees the spirituality of the married state as a mirror of the relation of God and the soul.

[11] For a study of medieval attitudes towards leprosy, see S. N. Brody, *The Disease of
the Soul, Leprosy in Medieval Literature* (Ithaca: Cornell University Press, 1974).

ask him during that period (*ST,* Suppl., q. 64, a. 3 and 4). The very different moral standards that apply to the two sexes are also evident in Thomas' remarks about adultery. Though unlawful for both sexes, it too is worse for the woman because of the offspring. The reason Thomas gives, however, for a man's right to divorce his adulterous wife (although a wife may not divorce an adulterous husband) is not the children, but the fact that divorce is permitted in order to avoid murder, and a man is more likely to commit murder than a woman (*ST,* Suppl., q. 62, a. 4).

With Bonaventure, we move into a different area; as a mystic, he deals primarily with the immediate relation of the soul and God. As one would expect, the emphasis on love and the union with God involves him in an identification with women and woman's role (cf. Bernard, Chapter One). It is not that his basic assumptions about men and women differ markedly from those of Aquinas—Bonaventure too speaks of the male sex excelling the female, as much in dignity of principle as in power of action and authority of precedence (Sent., Bk. III, D. XII, a. iii, q. 1), and he describes the female sex as the flesh, a servant maid always willing to give access as Eve did (Coll., 17th, 16).[12] But he does not share Aquinas' devotion to Aristotle, whom he criticizes for attacking Plato, calling Aristotle's arguments worthless (Coll., 6th, 2). Sometimes he directly disagrees with both Aquinas and Aristotle. Whereas they contend that the mother has only a passive power in conception, Bonaventure insists that she also has an active power, which is why some children resemble their mothers more than their fathers (Sent., Bk. III, D. IV, a. iii, q. 1). And Bonaventure argues that the Virgin had more than passive power in Christ's conception.

The language Bonaventure adopts about nature and the universe, his use of birth imagery, is more neo-Platonic (cf. Chartrians, Chapter Two) than Aristotelian. He speaks of the heavenly hierarchy

---

[12] Cf. *Apologia Pauperum,* V, 13: "women who cater to the flesh partake of it, their passion overflows in the sexual act . . . those whose womb carries progeny, their belly also is filled with meat." (Text based on Vinck translation.)

conceiving principles of predestination from eternity; as it conceived them, so it produced or bore them in time and gave birth to them by suffering in the flesh (Coll., 20, 5). Eternal Wisdom is spoken of as a woman, he explains, not because wisdom is effeminate, but because a principle of fecundity operates in the conceiving, the bearing and bringing forth of everything that pertains to the universality of laws (ibid.). The two sexes are one aspect of God's twofold creation; man himself is formed of two completely opposite principles (body and soul) combined in a single person. He has twofold perception (interior of mind, exterior of flesh), twofold command (nature and discipline), two books (God's Wisdom and the perceptible world), and twofold goods (visible and invisible, temporal and eternal, carnal and spiritual) (Brev., II, 10, 3 and 11, 1 to 5). Bonaventure can still conceive of woman as a part of man—or perhaps it would be better to say, can conceive of a part of man as woman—and she is the part that is most receptive to God. The soul is the bride, daughter, sister, and beloved of God (*Vitis Mystica,* III, 5; *Itinerarium Mentis,* IV, 8). In a dialogue between the soul and reason, Bonaventure has reason (also called the inner man and the conscience) prepare the soul for her union with God; reason teaches her, but it is the soul, with her capacity for love, that will achieve the union (*Soliloquium de quattuor mentalibus exercitiis*). If the soul is faithful to God, she will give birth to progeny of good works (*V.M.* III, 5), or even to Christ himself (*De quinque fest. p. Jesu,* I, 7).

It is tempting to speculate that Bonaventure's concern with union and love makes him more sympathetic to the union of man and woman than Thomas. In Bonaventure's view, man and woman have something to offer each other in marriage beyond progeny: they were made to be joined together, to comfort each other (hence Eve was taken from Adam while he was asleep), to be sustained by one another (hence from his bone), and to have a certain equality and mutuality (hence from his side) (Sent., Bk. II, D. XVIII, a. 1, q. 2). Like Hugh, Bonaventure speaks of marriage as a sacrament that existed before the fall; originally a symbol of the union of God and the soul, it now signifies the union of Christ and the church and of the two natures in one person (Brev. VI, 13).

Certainly Bonaventure identifies women with love, and therefore identifies himself with the women who loved God. He wishes to become the Virgin Mary and Mary Magdalene, in order to experience the compassion they felt at Christ's crucifixion (*Lignum Vitae,* II, 32). For Bonaventure, Mary Magdalene is the type of the repentant sinner. Though he associates her with Paul, as two who had lived in sin and then turned to God, he makes more of Mary's conversion, pointing out that she was quickly permitted to sit at Christ's feet among the holy apostles, and that she deserved to be the first to see Him after the resurrection, thenceforth never ceasing to impart words of truth to others. Bonaventure seems to have no objection to her teaching. Her devotion was so intense, "such fervor burned in her heart, such sweet pity inundated her, such strong bonds of love drew her, that womanly weakness was forgotten and neither darkness of night nor the brutality of the persecutors could keep her from the tomb—*even the disciples had fled, yet she did not flee*" (*Lignum Vitae,* II, 32, italics mine). Bonaventure does not explain, as the *Gloss* and Aquinas do, that women were the first to see the risen Christ because they had been the first to fall; rather, it was a favor they earned by the greatness of their love (*L.V.,* III, 34).

Bonaventure does not shrink from using women as examples of mankind saved (*L.V.,* I, 11 and 13), or of virtues (*Coll.* 7th, 18). The contemplative soul is represented by a woman, called the daughter of Jerusalem, because she is beautiful and fruitful (*Coll.* 20th, 6). The church is another Esther, lifted up among nations as the mother, queen, and teacher. Indeed, Bonaventure sees the stages of the soul's purification as women: if you cannot be a Catherine or Cecilia (an innocent), he urges, do not disdain to be a Mary Magdalene or a Mary of Egypt (a repentant sinner), and finally you may become a Mary, mother of God (*De q. fest. p. Jesu,* I, 7). In order to bear Christ in the soul, man must first become Mary for Mary is not only the glorification of humanity and the mirror of all virtues (*L.V.,* IV, 2), she is the gate of heaven essential to man's salvation. The lord never receives anyone except through her (*De Assuntione BVM,* VI, ix).[13] She is the mediator between us and Christ, as Christ is between us and God (Sent. Bk. III, D. III, q. i, a. 1). She is an active force in our salvation as she was an active force in the conception of her son. She became a mother in the most complete sense, without man, because the love of the Holy Spirit burned so intensely in her soul that the powers of the Holy Spirit wrought marvels in her flesh (Brev. IV, 3). And, equally striking in contrast to Aquinas, Bonaventure notes that Mary is the only witness to the Incarnation and to other early mysteries; it is from her testimony that accounts of the early life come. The faith which the apostles preached depends on her declaration (*De Assuntione BVM,* VI, ix).

It is clear from the differences between Aquinas and Bonaventure that it is not religion that determines the positive or negative attitude towards women, but the nature of the religious impulse; the philosopher-moralist tends to be antifeminist in attitude and imagery, the mystic does not. In the *Roman de la Rose* (at least in the bulk of it, which is by Jean de Meun), the philosopher-moralist dominates and we have a view of love between the sexes that is quite similar to that of Thomas. The only reason for sexual intercourse is procreation; any other involvement with women is dangerous.

Guillaume de Lorris, who began the poem, does not have Jean's wide scope; he is concerned only with the kind of love that is a literary phenomenon. His avowed reason for writing is to win the favor of his own lady, so worthy of love, he claims, that she should be called Rose. His love narrative pretends to be a description of the lover's torment and desires, a complaint about the lady's treatment, meant to elicit her favor or mercy much as the shorter lyric poem would. The *Roman* is an extension of the lyric situation, an analysis of its psychology. However, the analysis reveals the hypocrisy, the self-indulgence, and self-delusion inherent in the lover's stance. He lays

[13] The interesting passages in *De Assuntione* are noted and discussed by E. M. Healy, *Woman according to Saint Bonaventure* (New York: Georgian Press, 1955).

claim to a lofty devotion, but he really cares only about physical possession, for he is never satisfied with what Bel Acueill grants him; he
always wants more. He consistently refuses to face the truth about
himself or his love: he thinks he knows how to look into the fountain
of Narcissus without risk, but in fact he sees only what he wants to
see. He even twists the point of the Narcissus story, drawing a moral
for ladies that they should not disdain their lovers, i.e., that they
should save their lovers from themselves. When Reson tries to do just
that for him, however, to counter his desires with truth, he refuses to
listen to her. He knows that she is the image of God, meant to keep
men from folly *if they believe her* (2974–79),[14] but he does not want
to believe, he wants to love. And so he turns to Amis who tells him
just what he wants to hear, who encourages him and gives voice to the
deceptive stratagems which the lover is not ready to utter himself but
is willing to act on. The lover is manipulated by Amis and by the God
of Love because he chooses to be. Amors is the son of Venus (that is,
the formalized game of love is born of lust); he is also the voice of
love within the lover, the lust that is disguised in courtly behavior.
The entire impulse to love comes from inside the lover—the lady is
only a passive rose when he swears allegiance to Amors, even the
arrows of her beauty are shot by the God of Love—but when anything
goes wrong he blames others, never himself. He blames the fountain
of Narcissus for deceiving him, though he thought he knew what he
was doing when he looked into it; he blames Male Boche for depriving
him of his lady, though it was his precipitous kiss that Male Boche
broadcast; and he laments his own misfortune, when Bel Acueill is
imprisoned.

In a sense, the poet shows the lover drawn in different directions by two women, Reson and the Rose. Reson tells him the truth
about his love, that it was the result of idleness (Oiseuse let him into
the garden), and that it is a folly that keeps him from better things. By
the lover's own admission we know that Reson is beautiful and that

---

[14] Guillaume de Lorris et Jean de Meun, *Le Roman de la Rose,* ed. F. Lecoy, *CFMA,* 3
vol. (Paris: Champion, 1965, 1966, 1970). Characters' names follow this edition.

her function is to guard him from folly, but he rejects her for the Rose, the woman who fits his idea of love. There is no contest between Reson and the Rose because the lover has already committed himself to Love; the debate between reason and passion is really between reason and the lover, who embodies Amors in himself. This is a significant shift from earlier courtly literature. An equally interesting change is the importance given the conflict in the woman. Although there is no suspense about the final outcome, since all her defences give way when lust (Venus) appears, still, considerable attention is given to the struggle between those qualities in her that are receptive to the lover (Bel Acueill, Pitié, Franchise) and those that oppose him (Dangier, Jalousie, Honte, Poor). Those that he comes into direct contact with, Bel Acueill and Dangier, are both male: Bel Acueill, because he is that aspect of the woman that plays the courtly game on the man's terms, the image of the man which he has projected onto the lady; Dangier, because he represents the strength she possesses to repel the lover's attack.[15] Both of them are pictured as the lover sees them: Bel Acueill as a handsome squire, because he cannot say no to the lover; Dangier as an ugly peasant, because he sends the lover away. The other qualities of the lady are female because they are normally associated with womanly behavior: Honte and Poor, fear of reputation and physical fear, on one side; Franchise and Pitié, openness and mercy, on the other; and, most effective of all, lust, or Venus. The woman, in other words, is conceived of as basically receptive, either through lust or compassion, but she is restrained by fear of the consequences.

The man cannot be said to experience conflict—he rejects Reson without a second thought and she is the only one among his qualities who opposes his love—but he too has both male and female qualities. It is the effeminate side of his nature that makes him vulner-

[15] Male Boche (slander) is also masculine because he represents the *losenger* (see l. 3551), the men who tell what they see; he is included among her qualities because her action gives rise to him and she fears his effect.

able to love: his leisure, or idleness, Oiseuse, pictured as a lovely girl who spends her time admiring herself in a mirror (suggesting vanity), and Courtoisie, the rather artificial code of behavior he practices. These he sees as young and lovely, while the qualities he considers detrimental to love—Haine, Vilanie, Covoitise, Envie, Tristesce, Vielleice, Papelardie, and Povreté—are depicted as old, ugly, and often mad women; the lover sees them as paintings on the wall outside the garden, not recognizing that they lurk inside him, and that his pursuit of love will bring them out. The only good female quality in him is Reson, whom he rejects for Amors. Amors is a masculine figure in this work because he represents the formalized code of love that man has fashioned in order to disguise his lust. The lover cannot face the Venus in himself; he must see her in the guise of Amors, with complicated rules of allegiance and patterns of behavior.[16]

When Jean picks up the poem, he continues the exposure of hypocrisy and self-indulgence in the lover and the psychomachia in the lady, but he expands the scope of both. The lover's quest is set against larger intellectual and philosophic views of love, with a second and more extensive speech by Reson and the introduction of Nature and Genyus and their arguments. The woman's conflict is expanded by the addition of new qualities which do not change the nature of the struggle [17] but reinforce Jean's view of it. First of all, they make the pro-love forces twice as numerous as the anti-love group. Since the latter are the more successful in battle and would have won were it not for Venus' arrow, their defeat serves to heighten our sense of Venus' power over the woman. Secondly, they are paired off (alongside the

---

[16] Guillaume exposes courtly love as a game that men play for their own satisfaction, although it is ostensibly set up to serve ladies. In fact, women often see through its pretences, e.g., the dialogues in Andreas Capellanus' *De arte honeste amandi,* and the questions Florentine ladies put to Dante about his love in the *Vita Nuova.*

[17] Delit, Bien Celer, Seurtez, and Hardemenz reinforce traits already there. Faus Semblant and Atenance Contrainte make the lover's deception blatant and make the rose an accomplice to it, but they are still part of the reputation-versus-desire opposition.

original pro-love figures) against the original anti-love qualities, in a clearly conscious balancing of male-female combinations.[18] The anti-love forces are the original four guarding the gates of the tower Jalousie had built to imprison Bel Aceuill: Poor (f), Dangier (M), Honte (f), and Male Boche (m). They are opposed thus: Seurtez (f) and Hardemenz (m) against Poor (f); Franchise (f) and Pitié (f) against Dangier (m); Delit (m) and Bien Celer (m) against Honte (f); and Faus Semblant (m) and Atenance Contrainte (f) against Male Boche (m). Thus Jean offers every possible combination of male-female except all male or all female, the four possibilities of discord, but not the two of concord. Only Venus' arrow, the sexual act, can bring the woman into temporary concord by routing the opposing forces.

Until Venus' intervention, the lady's struggle is essentially between fear for her reputation and her desire to indulge the man and herself. She is not concerned with moral issues or with the lover's plight. Only Pitié really feels for him, and her effect on Dangier is quickly offset by Honte, fear of her reputation. Though she is too young to feel the need for money, as la Vielle urges, she is calculating in other ways. In the person of Bel Acueill, she is careful what she says to la Vielle. She does not reveal her own desires, but flatters the old woman, and she is cautious about accepting gifts from the lover until la Vielle offers a cover-up story. It is only after Male Boche is treacherously murdered (by Faus Semblant, false appearance) that the pro-love forces can make their attack. When the battle is over and Bel Acueill gives the lover the rose, he says "bien voi quil aime sans guile" (21315: I see clearly that he loves without guile), such a patently false statement that it cannot be taken seriously. It seems more likely that the lady, having given in to love, will now adopt the same sort of veneer the lover has used, and pretend that they share a noble sentiment. It is, the poet tells us, her first experience, though he does not think it will be the last (21630 ff). She has taken her first step towards becoming a Vielle.

[18] I am indebted to a graduate student at Columbia University, Mr. Stewart Justman, for revealing the structure of this opposition.

The man struggles meanwhile to justify his lust by fitting it into a larger context. Amors does not really serve the purpose. Indeed, for all the lover's boasted loyalty to him, Amors has little effect on the events in Jean's poem—he can do no more than summon his mother. The lover must find a way to answer Reson's strong arguments against his love, and he does so through Nature's and Genyus' exhortations to procreate; he justifies his sexual urge with the claim that he is serving Nature's and God's purpose, although in fact it is pure accident that he plants the seed at all. (When he dislodges the bud, he spills the seed and some of it happens to take.) Reson is brought back into the poem at the beginning of Jean's part. When the lover is temporarily disillusioned with Amors (only because he has been stymied in his pursuit), his doubts open his mind to Reson once again. But since he is still unable to free himself from Love, he remains Love's spokesman in the debate. Reson is a separate and alien figure whose arguments he does not really consider. What she says is both true and reasonable, that the highest love is charity or friendship, selfless devotion, but natural love, if it is for procreation, is also acceptable; the only sinful love is for gain, and that is what the lover is engaged in. His illogical answers to her reveal how far he has removed himself from the rational sphere. When she tells him he would not have become Love's man had he known what Love was, he answers, "I know him because he said I should be happy to have such a good master" (4225–27). When he has no other reply, he seizes on her use of the word *coilles,* accusing her of being unladylike and uncourtly (6899 ff). He cannot face the fact baldly stated, though his actions reveal his own obsession with it. When she offers herself as a more suitable lover, he rejects her with a reference to Echo. In his usual limited way, he sees only the surface analogy of the rejected lady's embarrassment. He fails to see the far more telling comparison between himself and Narcissus. Narcissus virtually committed suicide by refusing Echo, and the lover does just this in a spiritual sense by refusing Reson.[19]

[19] Much later in the poem he will refer to the Pygmalion story, again because of the surface comparison, the beauty of the image, but he will fail to see the deeper connection.

Reson is rejected by the lover in no uncertain terms, but she is the only character in the poem who is not undercut by the author. Both Nature and Genyus make effective speeches—Nature about her continual war with death to preserve the created universe, Genyus about paradise and salvation—but both of them are ultimately tools of Venus. (It is conceivable that, since the seed *is* planted, however absent-mindedly, Nature's work is being done and God has the last laugh. But Jean seems to be saying that, in having sex for pleasure rather than for procreation, the lover is damning himself, whatever the immediate result of his act.) Genyus doffs his priestly robes when he goes to help Amors—the word used is *desafublez* (19401), as if they were an encumbrance—and is clothed by Amors in a chasuble and miter, with a ring and cross and a candle of non-virgin wax from the hand of Venus. Genyus attempts to disguise his moral purpose in the garb of the false religion as Faus Semblant had donned the robes of a true priest to disguise his treachery; both work to the same immediate end. Genyus has given himself over to the false religion: Love's company swears by quivers, bows, and arrows, their relics, in which, the poet comments, they believe as in the trinity. In a sense, these signs of idolatry raise doubts about the promise of salvation Genyus makes to justify the attack on the rose. He makes that promise knowing the sexual act will involve sin, advising them thus: "Embrace your love, and when you have played, confess and call on God" (19861–63). Once lust begins to work (when Venus spreads her flame), Genyus vanishes from the scene. He had come to rationalize lust, but he does not stay to see the deed through, and it is only by accident that it is accomplished.

Although he is Nature's priest, Genyus does not hide his con-

---

The description he gives of Pygmalion in love with a statue reads like a parody of the courtly lover: he is trapped by his own creation, he loves an image that cannot speak or show mercy, he can caress her but she is unresponsive; when he thinks her flesh moves, it is his own hand he feels; he worships her but he is not satisfied. He repents of his devotion to Chastity (perhaps the self-denying pose of the courtly lover) and prays to Venus to give life to the lady, just as in the poem it is lust that makes the lady receptive to the lover.

tempt for her because she is a woman. He first extends a formal greeting that befits her position: "ma dame, du monde raine/ cui toute riens
mondaine ancline" (16265–66: my lady, queen of the world, before
whom everything in the world bows). But he quickly puts her down:
"stop crying . . . women get upset over nothing;" and then launches
into an attack on women, citing notable authorities. When he leaves to
do her errand, he tells her to stay in her forge and keep working
(19389 ff)—woman's place is in the. . . . Nature is, to some extent,
worthy of his contempt: she is foolish in her trust of Amors believing
that he really works to serve her; she weeps in frustration when man
refuses to do her work; and she is vindictive about him and pleased at
the thought of his infernal punishments.[20] These actions hardly accord
with her learned discourse, or her acknowledgement of reason's importance in keeping man from sin. Of course it is true, as Fleming
points out, that after the fall Nature too is corrupt, that her attempt to
fight physical death leads to spiritual death, but it is also possible that
Jean is downgrading the divine goddesses of earlier works to mere
women.[21]

Venus, too, is more petty, though at the same time more evil,
than in Alanus' poems. But she is primarily a woman. She is vindictive in her feud with Chastee, Honte, and Reson; when she shoots the
arrow between the columns, she seems "fame courrouciee." The
story of her affair with Mars, which describes the awkward position in
which Vulcan caught them with his net, precedes her appearance in
the poem, so that from the beginning we think of her more as an adulterous woman than as a goddess, despite her powers. Through Faus

---

[20] "Mar s'est de moi tant estrangiez/ si vice i seront recité/ et dirai de tout verité"
(19192–94: "he'll be sorry he alienated himself from me, I'll tell the whole truth about
his vices"); 19284, "I'll be well avenged."

[21] J. V. Fleming, *The Roman de la Rose, A Study in Allegory and Iconography* (Princeton University Press, 1969), p. 194 ff. Economou, p. 110, notes that Nature never
refers to marriage, she worries only about procreation. [Gunn, *The Mirror of Love* (Lub-
bock: Texas Tech, 1952) see the ideas of each character in the debate as steps towards
the maturity of the lover, but I do not think this explains the mockery of figures like
Venus and Nature.]

Semblant, she is allied with the forces of Antichrist and false religion, and she does not scruple to draw Genyus, a vicar of the true God, into her service.

The attacks on women, generally, are frequent and fierce in Jean's portion of the poem. Women are condemned verbally by men (Amis and Mariz), by a woman (la Vielle), by personifications male (Genyus) and female (Nature), and tacitly by the behavior of Venus and Nature and of the rose. Only Reson does not attack women and that is because she sees the whole moral and philosophical picture; she places the blame where it belongs, on the individual who sins, male or female. Though the attacks of Amis and Mariz are reinforced by la Vielle's admissions, they are also counterbalanced by her remarks about men and undercut by Amis' and Mariz's descriptions of their own lives. Women are greedy and lustful, but men are selfish and tyrannical. Both Mariz and la Vielle agree that love must be free and that it cannot be free in marriage; since it cannot be sinless outside of marriage, we are left to conclude that sexual love must be rejected.

La Vielle's ideas are worth noting, as the one expression in the poem of what purports to be a woman's thought. She herself is an illustration of the strongest antifeminist diatribes; she sketches all the ways women can deceive and fleece and tyrannize men. But she excuses these deceptions with a plea for woman's freedom which, taken out of context and read from a modern, liberal point of view is attractive: marriage, she says, was set up to prevent wars and murders over women; but it thwarts nature, which did not intend one man for one woman or vice versa, but for all to be free. Because marriage robs them of their freedom, women expend their efforts to win it back. Of course, she admits that the devil gave women their cleverness (14408), and that women have poor judgment (14459). And her whole speech must be considered in the light of traditional teaching; first, that marriage was held by some to be the one sacrament that antedated the fall, and second, that it was precisely the desire to be free of God's restrictions that led to the fall. Thus, the freedom la Vielle seeks is the freedom to indulge her desires and deny her duty to God, and is therefore meant to be condemned. But it is an interesting outcry none-theless.

Jean is clearly less interested in the workings of love in the in-dividual than in the larger problems of *bone amor* or *bone volenté commune,* as it is expounded by Reson, and *fole amor,* the selfish pas-sion represented by Venus and abetted by Nature and Genyus because they think it can serve the cause of procreation (the same mistake Na-ture made in Alanus' *De planctu*). Jean is not as concerned with the contrast between *fole amor* and *fin amor,* the courtly or literary tradi-tion represented by Amors. Genyus enables the lover to disguise his sin; Amors only permits him to disguise his vulgarity. Behind the three kinds of love lie the theological and literary traditions we have alluded to in this and preceding chapters. The pure love that Reson offers, the basis of all good and justice in the universe, is impossible because man is too selfish. The poem does not really condemn women more than it does men; both are shown to be greedy, lustful, and deceptive by nature, but women seem to have little hope of being anything else. Men, if they heed the lesson of the poem and guard themselves against the seductions of love, if they at least recognize lust for what it is and do not delude themselves, may rise above their natures. What the poem shows is that man is seduced by his own desires; he is suscepti-ble to women and love only if he chooses to be. The woman does little or nothing to set off his emotion, but once he gives himself over to it he is in her power and no good can come of their relationship.

The vulgate cycle of Arthurian romances, in the final analysis, teaches the same lesson. Women are too dangerous to get involved with because men are too weak to withstand them, so the only safe life is one of chastity and abstinence. But the cycle is a vast body of mate-rial, made up of at least four separate romances, which one cannot reduce satisfactorily to a single attitude.[22] As in the *Roman de la*

---

[22] The four parts considered here appear in *The Vulgate Version of the Arthurian Ro-mances,* ed. H. O. Sommer, 5 vol. (Washington: Carnegie Institute, 1908, 1910, 1911, 1912); II, *L'Estoire de Merlin;* III–V, *Le Livre de Lancelot del Lac. La Queste del Saint Graal,* ed. A Pauphilet, *CFMA* (Paris: Champion, 1967). *La Mort Le Roi Artus,* ed. J.

Rose, there are conflicting traditions, in this case, the chivalric and the religious. The literary tradition of chivalry presents women as objects of and inspirations for noble activity, but in the context of the Grail quest women are worldly attractions that prevent the heroes from reaching their goal and from saving their souls. The vision Arthur has of Fortune, at the end of the cycle, might be taken as an emblem of woman in these romances: she appears as a beautiful lady, who had once been a mother to him, and then had become a step-mother (*Mort,* 172, ll. 49–50); she is seated on the highest portion of a wheel, but threatens him with destruction. So women are to Arthurian knights: beautiful on the surface, appearing to offer the highest goods, but ultimately disappointing and ruinous to the men who follow them.

Lancelot is the knight in whom we can best see this effect. His love for Guenievre inspires him to outstanding deeds and seems to provide what he needs in the world, but it prevents him from achieving the highest goal and finally leads to worldly dishonor and, at least partially, to the destruction of the society he had served. Lancelot, more than anyone else, is caught between the two codes of behavior. He is the finest knight of the Arthurian world until physical purity becomes a knight's most important quality. Because of his sinful love for the queen he cannot achieve the Grail, as she herself laments. And yet, he assures her, without that love he could not have achieved what he did. She enhanced his powers and gave him the heart to undertake adventures (*Lanc.,* Pt. III, 193). A hermit in the *Queste* will tell Lancelot that a devil took possession of Guenievre in order to lure him to his destruction, and that only God was responsible for whatever good he did (p. 125–26), but one cannot help feeling that this is a revisionist explanation, that the real tragedy of Lancelot is precisely that love for Guenievre made him the finest knight, and the same love prevented him from reaching a knight's highest goal. He does vow to renounce his love during the quest, but despite the vow he returns to

---

Frappier (Genève: Droz, 1964). References will be given in the text with abbreviated titles.

the queen, and from that point on the love takes on a sordid aspect, like most things in the Arthurian world after the quest. The queen is fifty, though still the most beautiful woman in the world; courtly conventions now work against the lovers, leading to misunderstandings; and they no longer exercise discretion when they meet, but carry on "folement." When they are discovered and almost caught, Lancelot flees, leaving the queen to be captured and disgraced (*Mort*, 90 ff). Returning to rescue her, he kills two of Gauvain's brothers (93 ff), setting off an enmity between himself and Gauvain that precludes any possibility of peace in the Arthurian world.

Seen in the context of the Grail quest, the love of Lancelot for Guenievre must be condemned, just as most women are condemned. On an adventure that demands physical and spiritual purity, women can only be a distraction. None but the men strong enough to reject them altogether can achieve the grail and salvation, the goal before which all the exploits of worldly knights become insignificant. It is not surprising, then, that women are revealed as devils in disguise. Not only is Guenievre said to have been possessed, but the women who tempt Perceval and Bors, trying to destroy their chastity so they will fail in the quest, are themselves devils; when they are rebuffed by the knights, they literally go up in smoke, leaving only a foul odor behind. The only good women in the *Queste* are virgins: those Galahad rescues in an early adventure, who symbolize the souls of the just; and Perceval's sister, who leads Galahad to the ship of faith. She is a Christ figure, in that she sacrifices herself to save a sinful woman so that when Galahad becomes her knight, he is dedicating himself to God.

The earlier romances in the cycle, *Merlin* and *Lancelot del Lac*,[23] offer a broader range of possibilities in women. There are innocent victims, the mothers of great men like Merlin and Arthur (se-

---

[23] "Earlier" refers to the narrative sequence; in fact, *Merlin* may be later than the other romances, see J. Frappier, "The Vulgate Cycle" in *Arthurian Literature in the Middle Ages,* ed. R. S. Loomis (Oxford: Clarendon, 1959). A. Micha, "The Vulgate Merlin," in the same volume, suggests that part of the *Merlin* was a prose redaction of Robert de Boron's romance and the rest a later continuation. All of the romances under discussion in this chapter fall within the period 1215–30, according to Frappier, p. 295.

duced by a devil and a man in the shape of their husbands), and the heroines of individual adventures (abused by men in various ways). Less innocent, but not necessarily evil, are the ladies whose love inspires knights, but may also cause them trouble. And finally there are sorceresses, women who deceive men to satisfy their own ambitions or desires or, worst of all, who use their special powers to dominate and destroy. There is one good sorceress, the Dame del Lac, who brings Lancelot up and uses her powers to help him; but she also encourages Guenievre's love for him, because it will further him in the world.

One of the prime responsibilities of the Round Table is the protection of women, who seem to need it. The world outside and sometimes inside the court is filled with men trying to rape virgins or seduce other men's ladies, plotting to steal their lands or marry them in order to control the lands. Women seem to be at the mercy of society, pawns in power plays, with little control over their holdings, their destinies, or their bodies. Even Guenievre is at the mercy of her husband; she is put aside by him and nearly tortured to death when he chooses to believe a false Guenievre. It is significant that Lancelot, who rescues her on this occasion, is not deceived by lust as Arthur is.

As long as knights are concerned with the protection of the helpless—essentially a worldly concern however noble—the chivalric ethic is maintained and championed, but when their attention shifts to the salvation of their souls, the chivalric code falls apart. In the *Queste,* one no longer has the sense of a society or fellowship of knights. Each knight is now intent on saving his own soul, even if it means denying his family: faced with the choice between rescuing his brother from certain death and saving a virgin from rape, Bors goes to the aid of the virgin because she calls on him in the name of God. Nowhere is the contrast between the chivalric and religious codes clearer than in Bors' temptations: told that twelve women will commit suicide because he refuses to love their lady, he chooses to let them lose their souls rather than endanger his own (*Queste,* 181). From a chivalric point of view, this is a villainously selfish argument, but, it turns out, he is right because they are all devils.

There is a hint of the devil's power even in the preceding romances of the cycle: most of the women with magic powers, including the Dame del Lac, were instructed by Merlin, whose father was a devil, so the line is direct. But the interesting point about the power of these women is that it works only on susceptible men. Lancelot, who remains true to the queen, is not vulnerable; he can undo a spell of Morgue's and resist Camille, who has captured most of Arthur's knights and the king himself. Arthur and Merlin, unlike Lancelot, are easy prey for such women. It is particularly interesting that Merlin, the wisest man in the world, should become the toy of a young girl. He falls in love with Vivien and teaches her all his secrets, led on by her flattery and promises without tangible reward, until she imprisons him for good. He has been too wise, throughout, not to know what she is up to, but too foolish to prevent her doing it. The man's willingness is the source of the woman's power; for all her magic, the man must come to her, must let himself be caught, before she can control him.

Arthur, embodying the weaknesses as well as the strengths of his worlds, is particularly vulnerable to such women. He is captured by an enemy Saxon, Camille (*Lanc.*, Pt. I, 406–27), because his physical desire overcomes his military caution. A Circe figure, she takes him prisoner and then systematically captures his knights as they come to rescue him. Only Lancelot refuses to accept her captivity; he goes mad and she releases him.[24] It is while Arthur is Camille's prisoner that Lancelot and Guenievre consummate their love, as if his lust opened the way to hers. Soon after Lancelot frees Arthur from Camille, the king falls into the power of the false Guenievre, who has come to

---

[24] Lancelot is cured by Guenievre and the Dame del Lac, with the help of a shield which keeps him quiet while he wears it, but which bothers him. The shield is a symbol of the love between him and the queen, which gives him sanity and virtue in the worldly sense, but which a deeper instinct makes him rebel against. The rebellion makes him seem mad, but it indicates that real sanity will come to him at the end when he repents and gives up the world.

usurp the place of the queen (*Lanc.*, Pt. II, 11 ff). She is the queen's half-sister, begotten by their father on his seneschal's wife the same night he begot the queen, a striking instance of excessive lust which is manifested in the physical resemblance of the two girls. The court is wary of the stranger's claims, but Arthur supports her, puts himself in her hands, and becomes her tool. To satisfy her, he puts away the queen, ignores his duties as king, loses honor in the world, and is excommunicated by the pope. Arthur's lust is what makes him such an easy target, and it will come back to haunt him at the end through Mordres, the bastard son he had begot on his sister.

Most of the women who exercise magic powers over men are able to control their own passions in order to dominate others, unlike the men who are their victims. Even Guenievre, who has no overt magic arts, exerts an influence over Lancelot's destiny. She arranges to see him, plotting private interviews while staging public encounters to throw off suspicion, and tells him what to say to Arthur. She takes some delight in his subjection (*Lanc.*, Pt. I, 262, and II, 220 ff), but she offers unfailing encouragement and devotion and she inspires him to deeds no one in his generation could equal. Within the courtly sphere, she is the ideal lady. Unfortunately, Lancelot should rise higher than that sphere, but he is held down by her love, a domination he willingly accepts. If the hermit in the *Queste* is right, Lancelot could have done far more without her inspiration than he did with it.

The Vulgate cycle, like the *Roman de la Rose,* finally condemns secular love between man and woman. Both works present such love not as a basic good that can be balanced with reason, but as a danger because it encourages selfish, worldly impulses. The cycle goes further than the *Roman* in discouraging all human bonds—not only sexual attraction, but family love and chivalric fellowship—and exalting virginity and total devotion to God as the ideal for men and women. This is an extreme but simple view which, given the basic weaknesses of men that both works demonstrate, may be the only ·solution.

Even the lyric poets of the *dolce stil nuovo* remove themselves in subtle ways from the sphere of secular love, while they pretend to be devoted to it. They believe in love as a good force and, like Bonaventure, in woman as the means of reaching God, but, like the *Roman* and the vulgate cycle, they seem wary of secular love as a good in itself. Their poetry is more intellectual and more scientifically analytical than that of earlier lyric schools. It is more stylized and less emotionally realistic than the Provençal poets we looked at in Chapter Three. The *stilnovisti* are far more self-conscious, but less self-aware. Whereas Provençal poets recognized in themselves the need for refinement through the adoration of a perfect creature, and at the same time the strong physical desire to go to bed with a receptive woman, the *stilnovisti* deal with the first need by making the woman a star or an angel with heavenly power, and cope with the other by analyzing the complex responses of their bodily organs. They retain many of the Provençal conventions, like the image of the lady in the man's mind and the man's inner conflicts, but in an exaggerated form. The lady, however, is not a projection of the man's values or needs; she is distinctly a separate entity, with greater powers but even less life. She is either God's instrument, by which he draws the man back to Himself, or an alien presence, an image which her beauty creates in his mind and leaves there to contemplate the turmoil it has unleashed in him.

Dante speaks of an image of the lady "up in his mind" (32, l. 44: su ne la mente),[25] beautiful and unconcerned, watching while his heart expires and his soul departs. The man's faculties cannot sustain the sight of the woman's beauty and so they are destroyed:

> Madonna, la beltà vostra infollìo
> sì li miei occhi, che menâr lo core
> a la battaglia ove l'ancise Amore

[Cino da Pistoia, XLV, 1–3] [26]

[25] Dante's lyrics are taken from *Dante's Lyric Poetry*, ed. and w. trans. and comm. by K. Foster and P. Boyde, 2 vol. (Oxford: Clarendon, 1967). The lyrics are discussed in this chapter, as part of the *dolce stil nuovo* tradition; the commentary in the *Vita Nuova* and the *Convivio* will be discussed in Chapter Five.

[26] The poems of the stilnovist poets other than Dante are taken from *La Poesia Lirica del Duecento*, ed. C. Salinari (Turin: Unione Tipografico-Editrice Torinese, 1951).

Lady, your beauty drove my eyes so mad that they
led my heart into battle, where Love killed it.

and

La mia virtù si partì sconsolata
poi che lasciò lo core
a la battaglia ove madonna è stata:
la qual de li occhi suoi venne a ferire
di tal guisa ch'amore
ruppe tutt'i miei spiriti a fuggire.

Di questa donna non si può contare;
chè di tante bellezze adorna vene
che mente di quaggiù no la sostene

[Guido Cavalcanti, VIII, 9–17]

My force withdrew distressed / after it left my heart / at the battle
where my lady was: who, with her eyes, had struck / in such a way
that love / threw all my spirits into flight. / One cannot describe this
lady; she is so adorned with beauties / that the mind here below cannot
sustain her.

The light from her eyes can throw his mind into such chaos that it
even causes a confusion of identity:

Donna, da gli occhi tuoi par che si mova
un lume che mi passa entro la mente;
e quando *egli* è con *lei*, par che sovente
si metta nel disio ched i si trova.

[Dino Frescobaldi, V, 1–4, italics mine]

Lady, from your eyes, seems to come / a light that passes into my
mind; / and when *he* is with *her*, it seems that often / he mixes with
the desire that he finds there.

In the phrase "when he is with her," the "he" is the light from the
lady's eyes; "her" refers to the poet's mind, where the light creates an
image of a wolf (*loba*, fem.) that terrorizes his body, putting his spirits
to flight. Thus, as the pronouns of line three anticipate with the rever-

sal of sex, the woman takes possession of the man; he surrenders his being to her, which he can do only by giving up his life.[27]

A similar struggle between Love (masc. in Italian) and the man's soul or life-force (*anima,* fem.) is common in stilnovist lyrics. Love in the man works to establish the woman's presence and power and to control his life against his own life-force. That is, the woman he loves destroys the woman that is his life: e.g., in Cino (LII, 2–4), Love holds the man's soul bound in his dead heart, and beats her; and in LXV and XLV, 1. 7, when the lady takes over the man's mind and threatens his heart, the soul tries to flee, but Love holds her back. Dante speaks of his soul (fem.) as married to his heart (masc.) but driven away by Love (masc.), which has almost killed his heart.

All the poets speak of the effect of love in terms of the movements of "spiriti," which Foster and Boyde call "the carriers of psycho-physical life." [28] The most exaggerated example, though probably not entirely serious, is Guido Cavalcanti's *Per gli occhi fere un spirito sottile,* XXII, in which "spirito" or "spiritello" appears at least once in each line. The concept of the various spirits that carry the reactions and messages of the man's faculties, all scattered in different directions as the man responds to the woman's appearance, heightens the sense of a fragmentation of his personality through love. Some of the spirits come from the lady through the eyes, most are aroused within the poet, but each seems to have a life of its own. Since most of them flee before the force of Love, the over-all effect is to weaken if not kill the lover: e.g., Gianni Alfani (I), whose heart has been taken away by a lady's eyes. The image of her greeting in his memory continues to terrify his eyes, causing his soul to encircle them with screams, while a gentle spirit says "look at her now or you will die." Death is a constant danger: in Cino, LXV, the lady tells the heart it

---

[27] Cf. XII, where Dino's mood is gentler but the effect is the same—the man gains peace by surrendering completely.

[28] *Dante's Lyric Poetry,* p. 52, notes to 14; cf. p. 80, notes to 27.

will die unless she, the lady, leaves; XXXIX, when the heart departs, Death, "that is, Love," which has killed the heart, remains in its place. Dino says the spirit of love in his heart tells him he should love death for the lady's sake (XVII, 31–33).

The invasion of the man's being by the woman's image, his surrender to Love, does not bring harmony, but chaos, and even death. The figurative death of the lover that is induced by Love and the lady is a negative effect of love, but the real death of the lady can have a positive effect, as Dante shows in the *Vita Nuova*. Her presence, in other words, whether as an image in his mind, or as a physical being he encounters (see *Vita Nuova,* Ch. XIV, Dante's instinctive reaction to Beatrice's presence), is disruptive to body and soul, but her influence from afar can be beneficial. The removal of the woman's presence leads the mind back to the essence of her beauty and ultimately to the source of that beauty, God. Dante speaks first of her beauty making God and heaven desire her (47, *Li occhi dolenti,* and 49, *Quantunque volte mi rimembra*), then of his sigh following her to heaven (57, *Oltre la spera*), and finally of his own journey to join her there (in the *Comedy*). Dante uses her death to build a system by which the woman can, literally as well as figuratively, draw the lover to God, but he is the only poet of this school to do so.

Other poets speak of similar powers in their ladies, but they do not remove their physical presence by death. Instead, they distance the lady by creating an aura about her that derives from her miraculous powers. She gives off a special light that makes the air tremble (Guido Cavalacanti, IV, 2), that rivals the sun (Guido C., II; Guido Guinizelli, IV). Her virtue dispels evil in those around her (Guido G., X; Lapo Gianni, IV; Dino, I, IX; Cino, XXXVI; Dante, 33, 35). To Dante she seems a thing come from heaven to reveal miracles (43). She may be a star (Dino, II, VIII, IX; Cino, VI) or an angel (Lapo, II, IV, VI, XII; Guido C., VI; Cino, XXVI) or both. Guido Guinizelli excuses himself rather playfully to God, saying "I thought she was an angel sent from you . . . it wasn't my fault if I loved her" (III, vi). But in the same poem he compares her seriously to a star, shining on the noble man who acts in response to her, to angelic intelligences, and implicitly even to God, when he says that the lady influences man as God commands the divine intelligences which turn the heavens. Elsewhere too the lady is compared, directly or indirectly, to God: in Lapo, XIV, "as the Magi were guided by the star to adore Christ, so Love guided me to see how humble and gentle she is"; and in XII, "as an angel becomes blessed only when it sees God, so I, being human, could become blessed here looking at the figure of this lady who has my heart." [29] Of course there is a good deal of hyperbole in these comparisons, but it is nonetheless significant that, if he would attribute beneficial effects to the woman, the poet must make her a supernatural being.

The lady may be the instrument of God or of Love, but she is not herself Love. Amore in the Italian lyrics is a masculine figure, a tendency that exists in the man which renders him vulnerable to the woman's influence, for good or ill. Love may even be the impulse in man that responds to God through the medium of the woman's beauty and goodness, but the woman is not a projection of the man's impulses; if anything, she is a reflection of God's goodness. It is almost as if, to counter the idea of woman as the tool of the devil which seems to have regained force in thirteenth century literature, and to save the object of their love and poetry, the *stilnovisti* had to make women the tools of God. In either case, women are separate entities, instruments of greater forces which work on man's inherent nobility or weakness to save or destroy him. The union of man and woman, whether literal or figurative, has little importance in this literature.

---

[29] Dante sees his lady preceded by Giovanna Primavera, as Christ was by John the Baptist, *Vita Nuova,* Ch. XXIV, although he does not see the analogy until he writes the commentary.

Chapter Five

Dante

Although he begins as a lyric poet within the same tradition, Dante moves beyond the *stilnovisti* in several significant ways. He turns outward beyond himself in order to understand the love he experiences, not just to acknowledge the beneficial effect of the woman, but to find a deeper significance in her existence and in his love for her. He is able to affirm secular love as the first stage of divine love: if a woman's beauty reflects heavenly beauty, if her powers to refine man come from God, then it is by seeking the source of her beauty, not by rejecting her, that man should reach God. Dante accepts the attraction he feels to physical beauty and ascribes it to the reflection of a higher beauty, so that he is able to preserve his love for a woman without letting it come into conflict with his love for God. In Paradise, he suggests that man can perceive the divine light only through the mediation of woman—until the end of his journey, Dante's eyes cannot bear the divine light except as it is reflected in Beatrice's eyes.

It is the beauty which appears in a wise woman, the spiritual beauty reflected in her physical appearance, which first awakens the love that lies dormant in the noble heart: [1]

> Amor e'l cor gentil son una cosa
>
> Bieltate appare in saggia donna pui
> che piace a gli occhi sì, che dentro al core
> nasce un disio de la cosa piacente;
> . . . . .

[1] Cf. Paradise III, 1; Beatrice is the sun that first awakens the love that ends in God: "Quel sol che pria d'amor mi scaldò il petto." *La Divina Commedia,* ed. N. Sapegno (Milano: Ricciardi, 1957); all subsequent references will be to this edition.

che fa svegliar lo spirito d'Amore
E simil face in donna omo valente.

[34 and *Vita Nuova*, XX] [2]

Love and the noble heart are one

Beauty then appears in a wise woman
which pleases the eyes so much that within the heart
is born a desire for the pleasing object;

it awakens the spirit of Love.
And a worthy man has the same effect on a woman.

It is not insignificant that a worthy man can arouse the same response
in a woman—the instinct to love what is pleasing and to desire what
one loves is common to all human beings and, if properly guided by
reason, will lead ultimately to God, who alone can fully satisfy human
desires.[3] Love is the spiritual uniting of the soul with the beloved object (*cosa amata*), of the lover with the beloved person (*persona
amata*), Dante explains in the *Convivio*. From such a union both parties profit—each communicates his qualities to the other.[4] What is unusual in Dante's view of love, particularly after the thirteenth century,
is that human love between man and woman is not just a figure for the
love of man and God, but a necessary step towards that love.[5] One

[2] The Italian text is from Foster and Boyde, *Dante's Lyric Poetry;* the translation is
based on theirs, with some changes. The same poem is found in the *Vita Nuova*, Ch.
XX.

[3] Love for the opposite sex is not the first desire one feels [see the *Convivio*, ed. G.
Busnelli and G. Vandelli, 2 vol. (Firenze: Le Monnier, 1954), IV, xii, 16], but it is the
first that can really be called love, the beginning of the emotion that will end in God.

[4] For relevant passages, see *Conv.* III, ii, 3; IV, i, 1; IV, i, 2. Cf. *Lyric* 83, first stanza:
Virtue was given to men, beauty to women; it is for love to make the two one.

[5] Dante also uses the marriage metaphor: in the *Convivio*, he compares the soul's marriage to God with Marzia's to Cato. Marzia stands for the human soul, temporarily
married to the body (her second husband) which dies; then she returns to God (Cato, her
first husband) (IV, xxviii, 14–16). Cf. Lyric 69, stanza vii, the marriage of the soul and
the body in life; after death, she returns to God as a bride. In *Convivio* III, xii, 5, Dante
applies the image to wisdom: Wisdom is in God in a perfect way, as if by eternal matrimony, whereas it is in the other intelligences in a lesser way, as if in a lover. In the

love does not cancel out the other; the one augments the other. In Purgatory, Virgil explains that love is not like the possession of material objects (the more one has, the less others can have); with love, the more one has, the more there is for all (canto XV).

Man reaches God through woman. Mary provides the way for all mankind, Beatrice for Dante. Together they enable Dante to see God: through Beatrice in the Earthly Paradise he will see the dual nature of Christ, the manifestation of God in time; through the Virgin he will see the trinity, outside time in the Empyrean. Women have both a symbolic and an active function in the salvation of man. At every stage of the upward journey they guide by love and prayer, by criticism and example. As reflections of God, as symbols of virtue and love, they draw out the good that is in man; as loving and compassionate beings, they bring the straying man back with their criticism, and help expiate his sins with their prayers. All women, not just the Virgin, can be intermediaries between God and man through love, moving man with their beauty and God with their prayers.

In the *Vita Nuova,* we see Dante guided by the understanding of women away from the selfish love of the early lyrics to the kind of love that will end in God. When Dante needs comfort and sympathy in his love, he instinctively turns to women.[6] After Beatrice dies and he needs to talk about her, it is only to women that he can speak, because he spoke to them of her while she was alive (XXXI, *Li occhi dolenti*). His faith in their understanding is justified by their perception of his problem. They are always aware of his suffering and give him the opportunity to relieve it, but they also alert him to what is wrong in his love and so set him on the right path. Noticing his vio-

---

Comedy, Dante will use the marriage metaphor for God and His church, for St. Francis and Poverty, and for St. Dominic and Faith.

[6] Other poets address the lady they love, but rarely other women; there are two exceptions, Guido Cavalcanti, who wrote his analysis of love apparently in answer to a woman's request, *Donna mi prega,* although he does not indicate that there is any friendship or understanding between them, and Gianni Alfani, who wrote one poem to ladies seeking comfort in his love, probably influenced by Dante (VI, *Poeti lirici*).

lent reaction to Beatrice, one of them asks to what end he loves his lady if he cannot bear her presence. He answers that he used to seek her greeting, until she denied it to him, but now he is content to praise her. Dante does not, however, deceive the lady with this answer as he deceives himself. If your happiness lies in praising her, she continues, why do you write about your own condition? [7] It is this comment that sets Dante thinking of love in a new way. He writes the canzone *Donne che avete intelletto d'amore*, addressed to ladies who understand love, in which God and the angels hint at Beatrice's purpose on earth (and even seem to anticipate the *Comedy:* "one who will say to the damned in Hell, I have seen the hope of the blessed," XIX). This lady's reproof, and Dante's shame, will be echoed with greater intensity in the Earthly Paradise, when Beatrice confronts Dante with his failures and compels him to face and to admit the truth.

Women's understanding of love is not confined to sympathy for the poet. They feel compassion for him because they are capable of experiencing the same kind of love themselves. What a wise woman can do for a man—awaken the love that sleeps in the noble heart—a worthy man can do for a woman (see *Amor e'l cor gentil*). Indeed, Dante reverses the traditional roles so that a man can act as intermediary with God for a woman: he can move God with his prayers for her soul, as Pier Pettinaio does for Sapia (Pg. XIII), the first example of the effectiveness of prayer that occurs in Purgatory. The presentation of woman as a complete human being, an intelligent companion rather than simply the reflection of a higher good, distinguishes Dante from the other writers discussed in this study (with the exception of Marie de France). When Dante says, at the end of the *Vita Nuova,* "io spero di dicer di lei quello che mai non fue detto d'alcuna" (XLII: I hope to say of her what has never been said about any woman), he means the glorification of Beatrice as the reflection of God, but in fact

---

[7] There is something of a tradition of women seeing through the hypocrisy of courtly conventions. See dialogues in Andreas Capellanus' *De arte honeste amandi,* and debates of Guittone d'Arezzo and his lady (particularly XXIV, XXXII, *Poeti lirici*).

he does something even more unusual for the dignity of women by presenting them as human beings.

Dante passes through several stages in his view of love and in his response to women, stages that can be traced through his works. He begins fairly conventionally in the lyrics with analyses of his emotions and his conflicts, looking inward and concentrating on his own suffering. His symptoms are typical: love causes him to tremble and faint in the presence of his lady; it sends his spirits scattering and makes him weep; it creates conflicts between his heart and soul. Sometimes the conventions of his tradition fail him: the poems he writes to another lady as a decoy to hide his love for Beatrice (in order to maintain the required secrecy), give rise to gossip which makes Beatrice withdraw her greeting from him. After Beatrice's death, even the poetic forms no longer serve: Dante begins poems which he cannot finish, or is dissatisfied with what he has done (see *VN:* XXVII, XXX-III, XXXIV, incomplete canzoni, false starts). He gives up writing about Beatrice at the end of the *Vita Nuova,* until he can find a new way to speak of her, a new mode, which the *Comedy* will provide.

Meanwhile, not yet understanding what love is, he looks to other women for the satisfaction he cannot have from Beatrice and yet must ultimately find only through her. The turning to other women not for comfort but for love is another convention of the lyric tradition which, as we have seen, reveals a conflict within the poet. Sometimes Dante dismisses the second woman: in *Per quella via che la bellezza corre* (*Lyric,* 58), a girl following the road by which beauty enters the mind to awaken love is stopped by a voice from the tower (Dante's mind); the voice tells her to go away, for another lady reigns there. Sometimes he tries to justify the existence of both women: in *Due donne in cima de la mente mia* (71), when two women argue about love in his mind, asking how one heart can be divided between two ladies with perfect love, he answers that one is beauty, whom he loves for the sake of delight, and the other is virtue, whom he loves for action. He pretends that he made another woman the subject of his

poems as a shield to keep his love for Beatrice secret (*VN,* V). The
most important of the other women,[8] judging from the lengths Dante
goes to to explain her away, is the *donna gentile,* the lady who offers
sympathy after the death of Beatrice. Her compassion unleashes his
tears, enabling him to wallow in his grief and return to the self-centered state of his early love. His attachment to her gives rise to a
conflict between those elements which find an outlet in her company,
his heart and desire, and those which are loyal to Beatrice, his soul
and reason. (*Core* and *appetito* are masculine, *anima* and *ragione* are
feminine, so it is the feminine side of Dante that remains true to the
right love.) Although his soul and reason prevail, Dante is apparently
not satisfied with the victory, for he feels obliged in the *Convivio* to
deny the existence of the *donna gentile* altogether by turning her into
an abstraction.

Dante's love for the *donna gentile* becomes a figure for his pursuit of wisdom, the studies he turned to after Beatrice died. The pursuit of wisdom is also a form of love: a "philosopher," Dante points
out, is not a wise man but a lover of wisdom (*Conv.,* III, xi, 5), so
philosophy is an amorous use of wisdom. Dante explains that he
imagined Philosophy as a lady because he could not write of her
otherwise in the vulgate (though he finds a way to do so in the long
commentaries of the *Convivio*) and because his audience would not
have believed in a love for philosophy as readily as in the love for a
woman. It is still difficult to believe in such a love when one reads the
poems, which are so full of conventional love-lyric elements. Boethius, who provided the model of Philosophy as a woman, does not
write love poems to her. If Dante's canzoni to the *donna gentile* are
poetic fictions, as he claims, then the literal meaning cannot be true
and an allegorical explanation must be found for every part. This puts
a dreadful burden on the poems. It is hard to believe that passages
about the fierce and disdainful lady refer to the poet's failing vision,
impaired by excessive study, or that the look of the lady's eyes and the

---

[8] There are still others, e.g., the *pargoletta,* 64, the *donna pietra,* 79, 80.

smile of her mouth are the demonstrations and persuasions of philosophy. Dante feels obliged to deny the *donna gentile* in the *Convivio*
because he is still thinking in terms of one-to-one symbolic relations:
if he loves Beatrice, he cannot love another woman; if Beatrice is
love, the *donna gentile* must be wisdom.

In a sense, Dante is making the same sort of error, only at a
higher level, in the commentaries of the *Convivio* that he made when
he was first attracted to the *donna gentile* in the *Vita Nuova*. Not being
fully aware of Beatrice's significance, he looked only for a superficial
satisfaction from her, hence he needed a substitute in a second woman
when he lost the first. He rejects the second lady in the *Convivio* by
denying her real existence and making her an abstraction, a figure of
Philosophy, but he will give up the personification in the *Comedy* to
return to a real woman, Beatrice, who is at the same time a personification. In a sense he admits the existence of the *donna gentile* in
the *Comedy* when Beatrice accuses him of forgetting her after she died
and giving himself to another (Pg. XXX, 126: "questi si tolse a me e
diessi altrui"). In fact, Beatrice absorbs the figure of Philosophy, for
she is Wisdom in the highest sense, when it is indistinguishable from
Love. Her explanations prepare Dante's mind, but it is her look and
her smile, not her demonstrations and persuasions—her love, not her
learning—which give him the power to ascend through the heavens.
Dante says in the *Convivio* that the same disposition that enables a
man to love enables him to follow wisdom, that those men who live
by their senses can neither fall in love nor have an apprehension of
Philosophy (III, xiii, 4). That is, he does not deny human love, simply
his love for another woman. In a way, his identification of the *donna
gentile* with Philosophy is a step towards his identification of Beatrice
with Christ in the fullest sense, as the Logos, as Theology and Faith.[9]

[9] What is said of Beatrice in this chapter does not pretend to be new; it represents the
points I consider essential to my general discussion. For extensive treatment of the figure of Beatrice, see C. S. Singleton, *An Essay on the Vita Nuova* (Cambridge: Harvard
University Press, 1958), and *Dante Studies, 2: Journey to Beatrice* (Cambridge: Harvard, 1967); see also C. Williams, *The Figure of Beatrice* (1943; repr. New York: Far-

Dante's problem with her was only that he did not go beyond the beauty and compassion of the woman he saw to the divine beauty she reflected; he did not, when he wrote the *Convivio,* see that all women finally lead back to God, when one is ready to see God.

But even in the commentary Dante wrote on his early poems, the *Vita Nuova,* one can see the direction he is moving in. The poems themselves are not very different from other stilnovist lyrics, but the explanations of their origin prepare us for the identification of Beatrice with Christ in the *Comedy.* The most obvious example is the vision he has of her death, with the portents in nature, and the angels singing Hosanna as they accompany her in her ascension (XXIII). After that vision, he sees Beatrice once more, preceded by Giovanna Primavera, as Christ was preceded by John the Baptist (he connects Primavera with *prima verrà,* he who will come first, XXIV). There are other hints: in her name, the one who beatifies; in her number, nine, whose root is based on the trinity; in the colors in which she first appears, red and white; and in the fact that her death gives him new life. But he begins to see her real significance and to follow her to God only when he can no longer see her (that is why he says that to speak of her death would be to praise himself, because she died to save him, XXVIII). In Purgatory (XXX, 121 ff), she describes how she sustained him while she was alive, but after her death, when she could not reach him through visions, she had to descend to Hell to summon Virgil; the coming in person, even to Hell, to save the sinner who refused to heed the divine message is another echo of Christ.

As he begins to associate Beatrice with God, Dante also begins to see Love, Amore, in a new light. His first impulse is to reject the Ovidian figure he has spoken of so often in his lyrics. Love is not a corporal substance, Dante suddenly declares (*VN,* XXV), but an accident in substance, a figure of speech with some truth behind it. In his

---

rar, Straus, and Cudahy, 1961). On Philosophy and the *donna gentile,* particularly, see E. Gilson, *Dante and Philosophy,* trans. D. Moore (New York: Sheed and Ward, 1949); although Gilson accepts the *donna gentile* as a symbol, he does not think she is set in opposition to Beatrice.

visions of Amore, Dante had suggested something more than the traditional God of Love; his words were spoken in Latin for greater dignity, often with overtones of the Christian God: *Ego dominus tuus*
(III), *Ego tamquam centrum circuli* (XII).[10] It is as if God had appeared to Dante in a form he would recognize and heed, that of
Amore, just as He appeared in a form that would attract him, that of
Beatrice. Dante begins to associate Amore with Beatrice after the
vision of her death, when Love tells him that anyone with subtle perception would call Beatrice Love because of the great resemblance she
bears to him. Dante had often seen Amore in Beatrice's eyes, but he
still treats the two of them as separate forces. It is only in the *Comedy,*
when Dante has come to understand that God is Love and Beatrice is a
reflection of God, that he can return to the figure of Amore without
embarrassment. Then he uses the very conventional images of Amore
drawing arms from Beatrice's eyes in order to strike him (Pg. XXXI,
116–17) and making a net of her eyes to catch him (Par. XXVIII,
11–12). In the same way, he can acknowledge the signs of the ''antica
fiamma'' without guilt, because they are all part of the same impulse
(XXX, 48).

   In the *Comedy,* Dante's major figures are complex symbols and
real people at the same time. Beatrice is Wisdom and Theology and
Christ, but she is also the Florentine woman Dante loved on earth and
the lady of the lyric tradition, whose appearance in the Earthly Paradise affects him as it did in life—he can hardly speak; he weeps,
hangs his head at her reproofs, and finally faints (Pg. XXX–XXXI).
She gives him his name, his identity, like the heroine of a courtly
romance. Her name has been the inspiration to move him through his
journey: when he is tired, it makes him climb (Pg., VI, 46), when he
is afraid, it draws him through the fire of lust (Pg., XXVII, 36).
Twelve lines of persuasion from Virgil do nothing, but the simple

[10] In the essay accompanying his revised translation of the *Vita Nuova,* Musa suggests
that Dante's God of Love has two aspects, one transcendent, the other worldly, and that
the two were often confused in Dante's mind and visions. *Dante's Vita Nuova,* translated and with an Essay by Mark Musa (Bloomington: Indiana University Press, 1973).

words "Tra Beatrice e te è questo muro" do all. Only his love for her gives him the will and courage to move. But she also forces him to see himself as he is, and to accept responsibility for what he has done. She inspired him to good on earth while she was alive, now she moves his mind to follow her to God. She raises him to the height of his powers and beyond (*transumanar,* Par. I, 70), to the vision of God and eternity that he remembers but cannot retain; it is she who "imparadises" his mind (Par. XXVIII, 3: "quella che imparadisa la mia mente"). In her eyes he sees first the dual nature, God-man, in the changing aspect of the gryphon (Pg., XXXI), and later the point of light with the nine circles around it on which all the visible universe depends (Par. XXVIII, 11–12). She is the continual source of his power, for it is through her eyes that he receives the reflected light of God which draws him upward.

Beatrice draws Dante towards God because she is Love, but she enables him to see because she is also Wisdom, Theology, and Contemplation. It is she who summons Virgil to show Dante the full extent of sin and virtue, appearing to Virgil like the lady of a stilnovist poem, her eyes shining more than stars, her speech angelic, so lovely he begs her to command him (Inf. II). Allegorically, the vision of the lady he loved appears in Dante's mind (represented by the figure of Virgil), and rouses it to look truthfully at itself. Virgil, insofar as he represents human reason and learning in Dante, can bring him only so far; he can teach only what logic can deduce. As he moves upwards through Purgatory he refers more and more to Beatrice, who must explain what he cannot. His wisdom is limited; hers is not, because she sees with God's light, that is, she understands through grace. Dante makes the figure that stands for his mind, for his reason and its limitations, masculine (he chooses Virgil, specifically, because he is *the* poet, and carries the full aura of classical learning). However, the figure who brings the light of true understanding, who introduces divine grace into his mind is a woman. In Beatrice's first and last appearances in the *Comedy,* she is seated beside Rachel, who represents Contemplation, the highest function of the human mind. That is the gift Beatrice bestows on Dante, the capacity to contemplate God directly.

As a figure of Wisdom and Theology, as well as the reflection of God in human form, Beatrice has similarities with Christ, which Dante intimated in the *Vita Nuova*. He carries this connection into the *Comedy*, particularly in the Earthly Paradise, where Beatrice appears after the figures who represent the books of the Bible, seated on the cart which is the church, and which she defends against its enemies. Her appearance is heralded by three shouts: *"Benedictus qui venis"* (Pg. XXX, 19), a clear reference to Christ, even retaining the masculine form; *"Veni, sponsa de Libano"* (XXX, 11), a reference to the bride of the Canticles, the church through which mankind is wed to Christ; and *"Manibus, oh, date lilia plenis"* (XXX, 21), a reference to the young Marcellus, who should have been Roman emperor. Thus Beatrice is associated with Christ in three ways: as the saviour, as the representative of all mankind, and as his regent on earth, the emperor. She tells her nymphs what Christ told his disciples, *"Modicum et non videbitis me"* (XXXIII, 10–12), and to save Dante, as Christ saved man, she descended to Hell: "soffristi per la mia salute/ in inferno lasciar le tue vestige," Dante says in his final praise (Par. XXXI, 79–81: "you were willing, for my salvation, to leave your traces in Hell").

Beatrice is the most important woman in the poem, the most directly concerned with Dante's salvation, but she works with and for the Virgin Mary. It is Mary who sends Beatrice to rouse Dante's mind, just as God sent Christ. The poem begins and ends with the Virgin, the mediatrix between man and God, the woman in whom all compassionate women are contained, the ultimate *"donna gentile,"* as Beatrice calls her (Inf. II, 94). Through her, Dante will see the trinity and within it Christ's human features, because Mary gave Christ those features. In Mary, one sees the closest human resemblance to Christ (Par. XXXII, 85–86); when Dante looks at her, he feels he has seen nothing so like God (l. 93). Up to this point, Dante has seen Christ only symbolically: in Beatrice herself, through Beatrice in the gryphon, and in the figures of the eagle and the cross. Mary has been

present as a force throughout Purgatory: she is the first example of the
remedial virtue on each level; in the Anti-Purgatory, the souls sing *Ave
Maria* (Pg. III) and *Salve Regina* (VII), and Mary sends the angels to
guard them from the serpent that tempts and threatens them. She is
both the model to follow in virtue and the source of mercy in sin. And
her presence dominates the end of Paradise as well: she is first seen in
XXIII as a rose, the principal flower in the garden of the church triumphant, where angels and saints sing *Regina coeli,* and where she and
Christ alone appear in their bodies (XXV, 127–28); and in the Empyrean, Dante sees all the souls of the blessed (the bride of Christ) as
one rose, her symbol (XXX).

Mary is the power which moves and completes the action. She
alone can dispose Dante to see Christ (Par. XXXII, 87). "He who
wants grace and does not come to you would have his desire fly
without wings," Bernard says in his prayer to her (Par. XXXIII,
13–15), echoing the words of his own sermon (In vigil. nativ.). She is
the queen of heaven, who can dispose things as she wishes: "Regina
che puoi/ ciò che tu vuoli" (Par. XXXIII, 34–35), Bernard says, making explicit what Virgil had often alluded to in Hell in order to open
the way for Dante (cf. Inf. III, 95–96, "vulosi così colà dove si puote/
ciò che si vuole"; also Inf. V, 23–24). Christ is called the "alto filio
di Dio e di Maria" (Par. XXIII, 136–37), as if the emperor and queen
ruled together. Mary is, in other words, the counterpart of God the father, but the female side of God, the mercy that can break harsh justice (Inf. II, 94–96). Mary, who is God in His power and mercy,
forms a female trinity with Beatrice (Christ and Wisdom) and Lucy
(the Holy Spirit and Love). Lucy is Dante's patron, a martyr described
in the *Legenda Aurea* as the temple of the Holy Spirit. Like the Holy
Spirit, she is a messenger, carrying Mary's request to Beatrice that she
save Dante, and carrying Dante to the gate of Purgatory. She appears
in his dream as a bird, a symbol of the Holy Spirit. The Holy Spirit is
Love, and Lucy, who moves Beatrice, is Love: Bernard says of Lucy
that "she moved your lady" (Par. XXXII, 137: "mosse la tua
donna"); Beatrice tells Virgil, "Love moved me" (Inf. II, 72; "Amor

mi mosse"). As the patron saint of eyesight, she also brings the grace
that helps Dante to see, to understand, and to endure the vision.

There is good precedent for the glorification of the Virgin in
the mystical writings of Bernard and Bonaventure, both of whom figure importantly in Dante's Paradise, and there is some precedent for a
trinity that includes female figures (in interpretations of pagan goddesses, see Appendix). But there is nothing to compare with Dante's
concept of a trinity of female figures who effect his salvation, all historical women—the mother of Christ, the third-century martyr, and the
thirteenth-century Florentine woman. What Dante says with this trinity
is that man learns to know God through a woman, that his desire to
become one with her can lead him to union with God, and that it is the
female side of God's nature that allows man to be saved. Beatrice
speaks of God in female terms, as "l'ultima salute," the ultimate salvation, in which Dante may "inher" himself (t'inlei) (Par. XXII,
124–27); cf. Par. VII, 142–44, "la somma beninanza." (In Par.
XXXIII, 100 ff, Dante describes God in the final vision as "quella
luce" and calls him "lei.") This goes far beyond the inspiration to
good deeds and virtue that a woman can be in courtly poetry; indeed it
solves the problem of secular limitations that such poetry raises by
making human love an essential step towards divine love and by making the woman he loves a reflection of God. And it suggests that in
His mercy and love—traits associated with women in the Bible and in
secular literature—God has a female side.[11]

It is not surprising, then, that Dante can also see female qualities in man as good. In the three realms of the *Comedy,* he uses a confusion of sexes to make a moral point, but not in the restricted way we
have seen in biblical exegesis. For Dante, it depends on the context. In
Hell, to be female is bad; it indicates weakness and insufficient moral
strength. In Purgatory, it is a desirable counterbalance to bad male
traits; and in Paradise, it indicates simply that there is no essential dis-

---

[11] God also has female offspring: Nature is his daughter, Art his granddaughter, according to *Inferno* XI; in *Convivio* II, xii, 9, Dante calls Philosophy God's daughter
("questa donna fu figlia di Dio").

tinction of sex in eternity—man can be spoken of as female, woman as male, all are saved. What Dante is concerned with is the essence of humanity which, like the essence of divinity, is both male and female.

The confusion of sex is part of the price souls pay for their sins in Hell, because they have succumbed to their lower impulses and surrendered to their weaknesses. When Dante first sees Ciacco, the glutton, he describes him as a shade, an "ombra," which is a feminine noun, and therefore he refers to him with feminine pronouns (Inf. VI, ll. 38–43: *ella, una, lei*). Even after Ciacco's speech, in which he uses a masculine adjective to describe himself ("disfatto" undone, is the word he uses), Dante fails to pick it up, and continues to speak as if he were female. Finally, Ciacco refers to himself as an "anima trista . . . non son sola" (l. 55). It is true that Dante is dealing with *anime* and *ombre*, which are necessarily feminine grammatically, but he uses the feminine pronouns to introduce only certain souls, leaving the reader uncertain for some time as to the sex of the person involved. That Dante intends this confusion to redound to the soul's shame seems likely from the care he takes to identify as men the people he particularly admires before any doubt can be raised. He speaks of Brunetto Latini as male (XV, 23) before he knows who he is, though he has just been talking of *anime* (there is, of course, an irony in this reference, since Brunetto denied his sex in his sexual tastes). He has Farinata speak before the pilgrim even sees him, using a masculine adjective (X, 27). In this case, Dante makes an interesting contrast between Farinata's awesome dignity and Cavalcanti's plaintive distress for his son, which is modeled on the lamentations of a woman, as Auerbach points out.[12] Dante speaks of Cavalcanti as "un ombra ... in ginocchie levata" (53–54: a shade, risen on her knees).

When confusion of sex occurs in Purgatory, it serves a different purpose from the shame it carries in Hell.[13] It is not a disgrace

---

[12] *Mimesis, The Representation of Reality in Western Literature,* trans. by W. Trask (1st ed. 1946; repr. Princeton University Press, 1953), p. 158.

[13] There is one probable exception to this: the souls of the slothful are called "anime donne," XIX, 51.

to be identified as or with women. Manfredi identifies himself by the good women in his family, his grandmother; Costanza, and his daughter.[14] He is described with feminine pronouns and adjectives (III, 79 ff: *lei, ella, pudica, onesta*) as he approaches Dante at the head of a group of souls that move like sheep. The analogy with sheep, like the feminine references, emphasizes the humility and gentleness that contrast so sharply with the furious warrior he was in life ("Orribil furon li peccati miei," l. 121: Horrible were my sins). His female side is good, and it is necessary to offset the violence of his life. Similarly, Sordello, who appears like Farinata, proud and disdainful, is described as an "anima ... sola soletta ... altera e disdegnosa" (VI, 58 ff). He is referred to in the feminine for eleven lines and Dante makes no effort to counter the effect. Guido Guinizelli is first referred to as "colei" (Pg. XXVI, 74), and later compared to a mother whose sons discover her burning (93 ff), but Dante finally calls him "father." Dante himself, like Manfredi, is identified with women in Purgatory; he is one who goes by the grace of a lady (XXVI, 59–60) and the one who wrote *Donne ch'avete intelletto d'amore* (XXIV, 51).

In Paradise the confusion of sex contributes to the sense of mankind as one, of the union or fusion of male and female. Piccarda, a woman, is addressed by Dante as "ben creato spirito," reversing the patterns of Hell and Purgatory; Cunizza is a "beato spirto" (Par. IX, 20). Boethius is described in female pronouns, like some of his companions in the sphere of the sun, though all of them were men; they are also compared to ladies in a dance (Par. X, 79). (Cf. John the Evangelist, Par. XXV, 103–4, who is likened to a "happy virgin" entering the dance.) In Paradise the sex of the soul depends on whether he or she is called *luce* (fem.) or *lume* (masc.), *anima* or *spirito,* apparently at random, indicating that sex matters little in this realm. Peter Damian, the contemplative (a state symbolically associated with

---

[14] There are symbolic overtones to this identification: Costanza means constancy, loyalty, faith; we will learn in Paradise that she was not sufficiently strong in maintaining her vows, but in contrast to her heretical son, Frederic, and her excommunicated grandson, Manfredi, she seems a pillar of faith.

women, e.g. Rachel, and Mary, the sister of Martha), is called "vita
beata" and "sacra lucerna," and addressed as female by Dante (XXI,
55–73).[15] He even describes himself at first with feminine words (1.
67), and only towards the end of his speech makes it clear that he was
a man (114–21). God, as we have noted, is "l'ultima salute" in whom
Dante "inhers" himself. Dante says of himself in relation to Beatrice,
"quella reverenza che s'*indonna* / di tutto me" (VII, 13–14). The
word *indonna* means "takes control of, rules over" (from *dominare*),
but the form, based on the word for "lady," is suggestive, particularly
since Dante says later on, in XXVII (ll. 88–89), "la mente in-
namorata, che *donnea* / con la mia donna sempre" (*donneare* means
"to behave like a lover"). They are odd verbs and Dante seems to
suggest by his use of them that he feels himself becoming one with
Beatrice.

The ambiguous use of pronouns is one of the most striking
ways Dante shows the fusion of male and female elements. But he
also adopts more traditional methods, as in the symbolic use of supernatural females, like harpies and sirens, and the identification of
women with specific sins and virtues. The Harpies provide a rather interesting variation on the motif of the soul as woman, in that in them it
is combined with the motif of the soul as bird.

The harpy-souls make their nests in the trees which are the
bodies of the suicides (Inf. XIII), an unnatural joining of soul and
body in those who unnaturally severed soul from body. The monster
soul continually attacks the body it was supposed to save. The sirens
are a conventional symbol of temptation, used as such by Dante in
Purgatory XXXI, 45, but treated unconventionally in the *femina balba*
and her echoes in the poem. The *femina balba* (Pg. XIX), who appears to Dante in a dream, ugly and deformed, represents the sins of
self-indulgence, avarice, gluttony, and lust. As Dante stares at her, his
look gives her life, speech, and finally beauty. That is, the man's will

---

[15] Cf. Charles Martel, the king, a "luce" (Par. VIII, 43 ff) and Folco, the poet-bishop,
a "gioia" and "letizia" (Par. IX, 37 and 67).

gives force to his desires—the siren can lead him astray only if he gives her power over him.[16] Dante counters the attraction of the siren with Lia, who appears in the next dream and represents the real beauty of the active life. Her words and rhymes echo the siren's, as a subtle indication of the contrast. The siren sings "Io son ... io son dolce serena" (XIX, 19), and uses *dismago, vago, appago,* as rhymes in her song (ll. 20–24); Lia sings "io mi son Lia" (XXVII, 101) and uses *smaga, vaga, appaga* (104–8). Beatrice, when she appears to Dante in the Earthly Paradise, not in a dream but in her real form, seems to echo the siren's repeated words in her "Ben son, ben son, Beatrice," emphasizing that hers is the beauty he should have followed, always, not just while her body was before him on earth.[17]

In the examples of specific sins and virtues, Dante is once again more conventional in Hell than in the other realms. There he associates women primarily with lust and deception (fraud), the sins traditionally connected with women in religious tradition. Lust is a sin that renders man effeminate, by encouraging him to indulge his desires at the cost of his duties. Dante shows this by presenting, in Canto V, a series of women who are also queens—Semiramide, Dido, Cleopatràs, Elena—all of whom abandoned their public responsibilities in order to satisfy their passions; the implication is that any man who gives himself to lust becomes a woman. When Francesca and Paolo appear, they

[16] Dorothy Sayers identifies this siren with Lilith [in her translation of the *Comedy,* 1955 (repr. Baltimore: Penguin Books, 1959–60), vol. II, p. 220]: "She is . . . the projection upon the outer world of something in the mind: the soul, falling in love with itself, perceives other people and things, not as they are, but as wish-fulfillments of its own. . . . The Siren is, in fact, the 'ancient witch' Lilith, the fabled first wife of Adam, who was not a real woman of flesh and blood, but a magical imago, begotten of Samael, the Evil One, to be a fantasm of Adam's own desires. (According to Rabbinical legend, God, seeing that "it was not good for man to be alone" with himself in this fashion, created Eve to be his true other, and to be loved and respected by him as a real person.)"

[17] A similar shift in the conventional figure, from sinful temptation to good temptation, can be seen in the apple, the sweet fruit which draws Dante to Beatrice, and not to sin (Pg., XXVII, 45 and 115), as he nears the Earthly Paradise where the other apple was eaten.

too reverse the expected roles: he stands by, weeping, while she narrates the story of their affair to Dante. Within the story there is another reversal: she wants Dante to think that Paolo made love to her, so she changes the details of the literary work she claims as the inspiration for their love so that the man, Lancelot, becomes the aggressor. In fact, as Musa has pointed out,[18] it was Guenevere who kissed him. Similarly, one must assume, Francesca was really the active force in her affair with Paolo.

The circle of fraud also has a female cast to it, particularly in the early sections, which have to do with satisfying the selfish and self-indulgent desires of others. The monster who represents fraud, Gerione, although it has the face of a just man, is spoken of only in female terms: as "a beast" (XVII, 1: "la fier"); "she who makes all the world stink" (XVII, 3: "colei che tutto il mondo appuzza"); "that filthy image of fraud" (7: "quella sozza imagine di froda"), etc., so that one must think of it as female. The first section of this circle is filled with pimps and seducers, men who exploit and abuse women for profit. But most of the women they betray had already betrayed others: Jason seduces and abandons Isifile, "the young girl who had first deceived all the others" (XVIII, 92–93), on an island where impious women had put all their men to death (89–90); he also betrays Medea who, although Dante does not mention it, had deceived her family in order to go off with her lover. In the same canto, but the next section, are the flatterers, a man and a woman. The woman is a literary figure, Taidè, portrayed as a symbol of the horrors of flattery: she is described as a whore who scratches herself with her shitty nails, alternately squatting and standing, reminding us of the connection between prostitution and flattery in biblical exegesis.

The third section of fraud is simony, in which the bride of Christ, the church, is prostituted by the greed of popes (XIX, 2–4, 56–57, 108). In this case the woman is the victim and the sin is treated as a perversion of love which is the gift of the Holy Spirit. In the

[18] See A. Hatcher and M. Musa, "The Kiss: *Inferno V* and the Old French Prose *Lancelot*," *Comp. Lit.*, 20 (1968), 97–109.

fourth section the false prophets are bisexual, the perverted use of their gifts making women of them: Tiresia changed all his members from male to female and then, by striking copulating serpents with his rod, returned to his manly feathers (XX, 45), a sarcastic reference to his beard and probably to other parts. Euripilo is said to have been an augur in Greece when Greece was void of males (1. 108), as if, by remaining there, he assumed a woman's role. The third classical prophet is Manto, herself a woman but seen here in a distorted female form, her hair covering her breasts on her twisted trunk (52–53).

With few exceptions, the rest of Hell is a male realm, whereas in Purgatory the female influence is felt strongly throughout, in itself an indication of Dante's unusual moral view. The light of Venus shines on the mountain of Purgatory in Canto I, and the power of love is felt thenceforth. Love is the basis of salvation in Purgatory, as distorted love is the basis on which the sins are divided (Pg. XVII). Love, for Dante, means woman, and thus women prevail here, furthering the salvation of men by example or by prayer.[19] They are present in various ways: as the illustrations of the virtues and vices that enclose each level; as the relatives whose prayers are sought by the souls; as the three heavenly women who guide Dante's journey; or as the symbolic figures he meets in the Earthly Paradise, Matelda and the nymphs. Woman's love binds man not only through sexual ties but through family ties, and the family is also an important element in Purgatory. Men look to their wives or daughters for the prayers that will help pay the debt incurred by their sins. Family ties also connect the souls with earth and bind the three realms together: Manfredi, in Purgatory, has a father in Hell, Frederic II, and a grand-mother in heaven, as well as a loving daughter on earth; Forese, in Purgatory,

---

[19] Anne Paolucci, "Women in the Political Love-Ethic of the *Divine Comedy and the Faerie Queene*," *Dante Studies*, 90 (1972), 139–53, makes the same point, p. 141: "Dante's plan . . . was to depict simultaneously the regeneration of man and the realization of world peace. In both, love is the irresistible force which gives impetus and meaning to human conduct on all levels, and Woman the natural embodiment of that force."

has a brother who is destined to go to Hell (see Pg., XXIV, 82 ff), a sister, Piccarda, who is in heaven, and a good wife on earth. (Note that in both cases the women are in heaven.) It is characteristic of the sense of balance in this *cantica* that there are such differences within families, that not all wives or daughters are good (Manfredi's daughter is good, Gherardo's is bad; Bonconte's wife has forgotten him, Forese's has shortened his time of penance with her prayers). Equality of sex is part of the balance, hence Dante has a woman helped by the prayers of a man, and men helped by the prayers of women. Contemporary women are as open to corruption as contemporary men, Forese points out, contrasting Florentine women of his day with his wife; but Cacciaguida, in Paradise, will praise Florentine women of the past as simple and virtuous, like their men.

The examples of virtues and vices that are presented to the eye or ear in each section are drawn from still earlier times, classical antiquity, or the Bible. Here too, there is a balance of male and female both good and bad: Mary is given as an example of every virtue, and she is usually paired with men, seldom with other women; the vices are shown in numerous examples, male and female, with men predominating.[20] But it is Mary's presence as an example of every virtue that creates the strongest impression of a female inspiration to good, which is born out in the Earthly Paradise by the seven nymphs who are the seven virtues. (They are not the same seven as the antidotes to the vices; the nymphs are the theological and cardinal virtues.) They have been seen all through Purgatory as stars (four in the day and three at night) but in the Earthly Paradise, where man is restored to a state of innocence, they appear as women. "Noi siam qui ninfe, e nel ciel siamo stelle," they tell Dante (Pg. XXXI, 106), a striking use of the lyric image of the lady as a star. In either form, they exert an influence over man for his good.

One cannot speak of the Earthly Paradise without thinking of

---

[20] There are two exceptions: no women are mentioned in sloth, but the souls are called "anime donne"; no women are named as examples of gluttony, but Dante thinks in his own mind of one.

Adam and Eve, who lost it for themselves and for mankind. Dante
thinks of Eve several times as he reaches the top of the mountain. (Her
existence has never been entirely forgotten in Purgatory: in VIII, 99,
she is mentioned in connection with the serpent; in XII, 10, the souls
of the proud are called sons of Eve.) Dante attacks her boldness, as the
only one who rebelled where all obeyed (XXIX, 24–27), and laments
all that she, the ancient mother, lost (XXX, 52, and XXXII, 32). The
heavenly procession seems more inclined to accuse Adam (XXXII,
37), whose name they utter as they approach the tree; this suggests
that Dante is making an error in blaming Eve, when he too should be
blaming Adam, that is, himself, for losing paradise through sin. In any
case, before he can rise to heaven, he must not only be purged of his
sins, but reunited with Eve, with the other part of himself, woman. He
meets a woman in the Earthly Paradise who will wash away his sins in
the river of Lethe. She is, among other things, a restored Eve, now the
only inhabitant of the Earthly Paradise—or the only one from Dante's
point of view. It may well be that, like Beatrice, Matelda would be
different for every man or woman who reached this point. It is Beatrice who names Matelda, almost at the end of her role in the poem.
Matelda, whose identity is left vague, intentionally I think, is a composite of various historical women and female ideals: both Lia and
Rachele, figures of the active and contemplative lives, whose appearance in Dante's dream foreshadows his meetings with Matelda; the
countess Matelda who served as mediatrix between pope and emperor,
a key function for Dante; perhaps the mystic Mateldas who wrote of
their visions of God; and Eve, the rightful inhabitant of the Earthly
Paradise—all these and perhaps more.[21] It is not by accident that her

---

[21] Singleton, *Journey to Beatrice,* Chapters XI and XII, suggests that she may also be
Astraea, Justice, which befits the ideal balance Dante strives for in Purgatory; R. Hollander, *Allegory in Dante's Commedia* (Princeton University, 1969), fn. 18, p. 152, discusses the possibility that Matelda's name is an acrostic, *ad laetam* spelled backwards.
E. Brown, ''Proserpina, Matelda, and the Pilgrim,'' *Dante Studies,* 89 (1971), 33–48,
presents the connections between Matelda and Proserpina. Hollander and Brown also
discuss the Eve analogies, as does A. B. Giamatti, *The Earthly Paradise and the Renaissance Epic* (Princeton University, 1966), Chapter II. And, in the compassion she

name is not revealed for five cantos, so that we are free to make of her
what we will; and, if she is a restored Eve, the more women she embodies, the better. Dante's meeting with her prepares him for his union
with Beatrice. He feels a desire to be with Matelda, expressed in terms
of Hero's desire for Leander, strong enough to make him swim the
Hellespont (XXVIII, 70 ff). This seems a more violent image than the
scene in the Earthly Paradise calls for but it is meant to emphasize the
power of Dante's emotion, which is sexual yet free of sin, as sex was
meant to be in paradise. When he sees Beatrice, two cantos later,
Dante feels the old flame but his love for her is now pure. He can rise
to heaven with her.

It is particularly significant that Dante's journey to paradise is
made in the company of a woman—mankind achieves perfection by
the reunion, in a state of restored innocence, of man and woman. This
union of male and female is essential to the order of Paradise, both as
a symbol of and a step towards the union of man with God. Union is
the basis of harmony in heaven. Although many of the souls Dante
meets here were committed to the celibate life, Dante finds ways to affirm human love. His love for Beatrice, and hers for him, dominates
the journey, which is climaxed by Bernard's love for the Virgin Mary.
The circle of Venus (love) is inhabited by men and women notorious
for their earthly loves, like Raab, the biblical prostitute, and Cunizza,
whose affair with the poet Sordello was a scandal of her day. Dante
does not choose the famous repentant prostitutes so often mentioned in
religious teaching, Mary Magdalene or Mary of Egypt, but women
known for the force of their devotion. "Mi vinse il lume d'esta
stella," Cunizza says (IX, 33). She who had several affairs is saved,
while Francesca, who had only one, is damned, because Francesca
was dominated by her selfish desires, Cunizza by a great capacity for
love. I do not, of course, deny the importance of repentance in the salvation of Raab or Cunizza (Folco, who appears in the same sphere,

---

shows for the poet, Matelda may reflect the *donna gentile* of the *Vita Nuova,* now leading Dante back to Beatrice, instead of distracting him from the thought of her. The
change has, of course, come about in Dante, not in the lady.

certainly changed his way of life from courtly poet to bishop). I simply want to emphasize that Dante is more concerned here with the force of love than with repentance. It is interesting, in light of this, that Cunizza and Raab are in a higher sphere than Piccarda and Costanza, two women who wished to remain virgins and who became nuns but were forcibly taken out of the cloister by their families and forced to marry. Their desires never wavered, we are told, but the force of their wills was lacking. This is why Dante thinks he sees reflections when he sees them—they lack substance—and it is why he places those who loved with great force of will, even if they loved men, above the would-be nuns.

What is important in all this is not that love is central to Dante's idea of Paradise—that goes without saying—but that earthly human love is a major part of love, a part which he does not deny even in heaven. In the circle of Venus Dante creates several new words to express the mystical union of separate beings: "s'inluia" (IX, 73), "m'intuassi," "t'inmii" (81), in this case to describe the union of Dante with the soul of Cunizza. That is, the force of love in this circle focuses Dante's desire on union, which is the final end of his journey. Dante uses the image of union between man and woman, namely marriage, to describe the ardor of two monastic saints and founders of orders, Francis and Dominic: Thomas Aquinas narrates at length and in passionate language Francis' love for Poverty, their marriage, and the fervor of his followers for his bride (XI); and Bonaventure describes Dominic's love for his bride, Faith (XII).

Behind these images lies the marriage of Christ and his church, a figure Dante uses mainly in his attacks on the abuses of the popes and the curia, their prostitution of God's bride. But in the Empyrean, he describes the rose as the bride of Christ. The rose is the figure of all mankind united in love; and in the rose we see the perfect balance of human elements, of Jews and Christians, adults and children, men and women, in overlapping halves. Children who died before the age of reason occupy the lower half, adults the upper; Christians are on one side, Jews on the other. Men and women alternate at all levels. For the most part, they seem to sit in vertical rows; all the souls seated beneath Mary are women, those seated beneath John the Baptist are men, but this does not hold true throughout, since Beatrice sits two seats below Peter. I have not found a clear pattern for the male-female arrangement, but judging from the number of individuals Dante points out in the rose, he does seem to intend an equal number of each sex, which would be consonant with the balance of the other parts. In any case, the vision Dante offers of mankind saved and glorified is a vision of the perfect integration of the human race with God and with itself. And Dante, a man, achieves that vision through the inspiration and active help of three women: Mary, through whom Christ brought salvation to all men; Lucy, the patron saint who cares for those devoted to her; and Beatrice, the lady Dante loved in life.

The integration of self, the completion of man through union with woman, which was a secular ideal in twelfth century literature and a religious ideal for a few theologians, is achieved here by Dante. For him, the integration is possible only in heaven, or in a vision, and only after the woman who inspires it is dead. Nonetheless, he achieves it not by rejecting the love of woman, as so much of thirteenth-century literature did, but by affirming and transforming it. (And, perhaps most startling of all in the context of this study, he offers the same possibility of perfection to woman.) Bernard and Bonaventure say it is only through Mary that man can reach God. Dante says it is through Mary and through human love for a real woman that he can achieve union with God. Beatrice may stand for many things, as the pilgrim Dante and his reader come slowly to see, but his first perception of her was as a living being, a beautiful woman, and it is because he saw *her,* that he came to see God.

Appendix

MEDIEVAL INTERPRETATIONS OF CLASSICAL TEXTS

Like biblical exegesis, which began among Hellenized Jews, the interpretation of secular texts has an ancient tradition. Homer was allegorized by the Greeks for moral and scientific truths from as early as the sixth century B.C. In the Middle Ages, scholars faced with a need to justify the study of pagan works, particularly those which dealt with pagan Gods, made such interpretations the rule. From Fulgentius in the sixth century A.D., who wrote on Virgil and Ovid, there is a steady stream that continues through the Middle Ages to the *Ovide moralisé* in the fourteenth century, and on into the Renaissance.

We can find many of the same attitudes in classical exegesis that were expressed in biblical commentaries (Chapter One). (There is, of course, a strong impetus to identify women with lust and carnal desires in the very nature of many myths.) In this tradition, as well, the word female is synonymous with weak and sinful. For example, after he loses Euridice, Orpheus scorns women, that is, "those living in the female way" or "the wicked," Arnulf explains, because "women are more prone to vice and desire," and so Orpheus devotes himself to males, "those acting in a virile way." (Cf. Fulgentius, *Mitologiarum libri tres:* "apud muliebres animos libido optineat regnum," "in womanish souls, the libido gains control.") [1] Self-indulgence is

[1] Arnulf, in *Arnolfo d'Orléans, Un Cultore di Ovidio nel secolo XII,* ed. F. Ghisalberti (Milano: Hoepli, 1932); Fulgentius, in *Opera,* ed. R. Helm (1898; repr. Stuttgart: Teubner, 1970). Most of the material covered in this Appendix, with the exception of Bernard's commentary on the *Aeneid* and that of John of Salisbury, is not available in English, hence I have given as many details as I could.

demonstrated only by women in the sixth book of the *Aeneid*, Bernard Silvester says in his commentary, because "the female represents the weakness of vice, the male the strength of virtue." [2]

But classical exegesis moves, occasionally, in a different direction: the stories are used not only as moral exempla but as scientific fables. The actions of the gods are said to reflect the course of nature in the seasons and even in the revolution of the heavens. Thus there is a double aspect to the material, a good as well as a bad implication to events and characters. Whereas the female figures are usually bad as moral forces, as cosmological forces they can be good. Venus, for example, can be either the benevolent planet and Goddess, whose influence brings harmony to the world and the universe,[3] or the destructive force of lust that undermines heroes and kingdoms. Guillaume de Conches interprets Venus' adultery with Mars in terms of the planets: when Venus is close to Mars she is less benevolent (*De phil. mundi*, II, xx); and she is connected with lust because the planet confers heat and wet, in which lust thrives. Bernard Silvester gives a long analysis of the two Venuses (in Comm. on *Aen*. I), one legitimate, the other wanton. The first is responsible for the music of the world and the equitable portioning of all things; in her role as universal harmony, or natural justice, she is the mother of Aeneas, the human spirit. The wanton Venus (concupiscence of the flesh) as the wife of Vulcan (natural heat) gives birth to Jocus and Cupid (sport and intercourse). It is often by the pairs of sons she produces that one sees the effect of her two natures. These pairs vary, depending on the source. Jocus and Cupid are her sons by Antigamus and Hymen, according to Alanus de Insulis in the *De planctu*. In his commentary on Martianus, Bernard

---

[2] Bernard's commentary: *Commentum Bernardi Silvestris super sex libros Eneidos Virgilii*, ed. W. Riedel (Griefswald: 1924); a translation has recently been done by D. C. Meerson, *The Ground and Nature of Literary Theory in Bernard Silvester's Twelfth Century Commentary on the Aeneid* (unpub. diss., University of Chicago, 1967). When I quote directly from the commentary, I use Mr. Meerson's words.

[3] On the tradition of the two Venuses in medieval literature, see G. Economou, "The Two Venuses and Courtly Love," *In Pursuit of Perfection*.

has Venus (desire) coupling with Bacchus (opulence) to produce Hymen (nuptial apparatus) and Cupid (love).

Lust, the life of desire, is by far the most common interpretation of Venus in the Middle Ages. When Venus has an affair with Mars, she is lust destroying the strong man, desire corrupting virtue with her embrace (Arnulf). She is born when Saturn throws the genitals of his father into the sea, thus she is the product of the male sexual organs, and it is on men that she has her effect. Her birth is sometimes interpreted physiologically, e.g., Guillaume on Macrobius: "the fruits of the earth, brought to maturity by heat, are cut off and collected and then thrown into the caves and craws of the human stomach, whence lust is born." [4] In the judgment of Paris, Venus represents the life of *voluptas,* desire, which Paris, the man of the senses, chooses over Juno, the active life, and Pallas-Minerva, the contemplative life or wisdom (Bernard on *Aen.* VI).

Pallas-Minerva is fairly consistent in her symbolic value; unlike Venus, she does not have a dual nature. She is always wisdom, always good, untainted by carnal desires, and free of sex, even in her birth. She springs from the head of Jove, born from God without a mother, as Guillaume puts it (Comm. on Macrob.), because only in God is there wisdom without the teaching and experience which are "the mother and principle of all wisdom in men." When Vulcan tries to make love to her she repulses him and his seed falls on the ground, producing Erictonius. For Fulgentius, Vulcan is the fire of fury, horrible vicious desire repulsed by the virginity he lusts for, which employs virtues as her weapon against him. In moral terms, Pallas is the wise man protecting himself from fury (Vulcan). In his commentary on the *Timaeus,* Guillaume identifies Pallas with wisdom, but says that Vulcan, who desires her, is the fervor of wit (*ingenium*)—natural, and not necessarily evil, concupiscence. Pallas is reluctant because no one can have perfect wisdom in this life. The seed scattered on the earth therefore produces a creature that is half man (with a rational concern

---

[4] Manuscript: Vatican Urbin. Lat. 1140, 2r-153v; the passage cited is found on 10r.

for the heavens), and half dragon (with a clever, practical concern for temporal things).[5]

Juno's symbolic life is more complex. She is both the active life (not in a religious sense, but simply worldly activity, power, ambition, wealth, in contrast to the life of the mind), and also the element, air. She is, of course, only the lower air, *aer,* not *aether,* which is Jupiter; Jupiter may be either higher air or fire, depending on the context. Air as Fulgentius notes, ought to be masculine. Juno is a sister to Jove in that she is a similar element, and a wife in that, as *aer,* she is inferior to fire or *aether.* As air, she facilitates childbirth with warmth and wetness (Bernard on *Aen.* I). As the active life, she is midway between Venus and Minerva, neither good nor bad but potentially harmful. She is a stepmother to Hercules, because the life of power is inimical to the wise man; wisdom (Hercules) impedes action (Juno), and works instead for good (Guillaume on Boethius, *Consolation*). When Ixion wants to couple with her, she puts a cloud between them and his seed falls on the earth, producing giants, because the active life obscures reason and makes men turn their attention to earthly things (ibid.). But Juno can also represent the divine will in a curious identification of pagan Gods with the three persons of the trinity: Jove is the power, which acts; Pallas is the divine wisdom, which disposes; and Juno is the divine will, which moves (Bernard on Martianus).

Generally, the classic myths lend themselves indiscriminately to either a scientific or a moral interpretation, and sometimes to both. The story of Tiresias, however, which is of some interest to this study because of his transformation from man to woman and back again, evokes only a scientific explanation. Fulgentius, Arnulf, Bernard, and the commentator in the *Ovide moralisé* all see in this story an allegory of the seasons. Tiresias is a man in the winter, when seeds are closed; when his staff (*virga* can mean staff or penis) strikes with fervor, he

---

[5] In Guillaume de Conches, *Glossae super Platonem,* ed. E. Jeauneau (Paris: Vrin, 1965).

becomes a woman, i.e., in the summer, when leaves and fruit emerge. The *Ovide moralisé* shifts the sexes.[6] Tiresias is male in spring when the seeds are growing, female in winter when they are dormant. This puts the emphasis on the male as the active force in reproduction, perhaps a reflection of Aristotelian views (see Chapter Four). The emphasis in all these interpretations has been shifted away from pleasure in love, which was the subject of the myth, to reproduction. No moral issue is raised.

This is not the case with most of the myths. Two of the most popular in the Middle Ages are the stories of Orpheus and Aeneas, each of which involves a love relationship with a woman, and the interpretations given them reveal the same assumptions that were evident in biblical exegesis. The Orpheus-Euridice story is made to sound very much like the story of Adam and Eve, where the woman plays the role of the lower, more susceptible part of human nature which falls easily prey to temptation and drags the higher part down with it. She is human judgment, which is poisoned by the fallacies of this world, the serpent. According to Bernard (*Aen.* VI), Euridice is natural concupiscence, who flees divine virtue, Aristaeus—a good example of the villain becoming virtue while the innocent victim is turned into the vice. In this version the serpent who bites Euridice is temporal goods. Guillaume de Conches (on Boethius, *Cons.*), also sees Euridice as natural concupiscence, married to every man like the *genium* that is born and dies in each of us; Euridice is both judgment (*boni judicatio*) and desire, in that we judge what is good and then desire it. Because she chooses temporal goods, she leads the soul to Hell. The interpretation that Boethius himself gives the story in the *Consolation* has none of the Adam-Eve overtones; in his version, Euridice is Orpheus' mind, which he must rescue from worldly interests. The *Ovide moralisé* adds another dimension: Orpheus represent Christ as well as controlled un-

---

[6] *Ovide moralisé, poéme du commencement du 14eme s.,* ed. C. de Boer, Verhendelingen der Koninkligke Akademie van Wetenscheppen te Amsterdam (Amsterdam: J. Müller) Vol. 15, 1915; Vol. 21, 1920; Vol. 30³, 1931; Vol. 37, 1936; Vol. 43, 1938.

derstanding, Euridice is still the sensuality of the soul, the shepherd is the virtue of living well, and Hell is the abysm of the evil heart.[7]

Aeneas, who symbolizes the human spirit, is subject to the same dangers of the flesh in the figure of Dido. This is true of most commentaries on the *Aeneid* (Fulgentius, Bernard Silvester, John of Salisbury),[8] but since Bernard's is the most extensive, I shall concentrate on it. As queen and ruler of a city, a woman ruling men, Dido represents lust that has overcome virtue. By leaving her, he lays his lust aside; lust then becomes weak and is consumed by the fervor of manhood when Dido is burnt on the funeral pyre. The women who later burn his ships are, similarly, carnal frailties which deny cooperation to the spirit and destroy the proper will with the flame of lust. In Book VI, the various aspects of self-indulgent lust are represented by women: Phaedra, Procris, Eriphyle, Evadne, Pasiphae, Laodamia, along with the image of Aeneas' own former lust, Dido. Self-indulgence is only represented by women, Bernard points out, because a woman's weakness and pliability is usually a sign of this fickle and enervating vice. Bernard manages to slip in a word on the self-indulgence of females even when he is discussing the Trojan horses (the horse may mean either the will or self-indulgence): Bernard cites Pliny's story of mares so lustful that when they cannot find stallions, they go up a mountain seeking the wind, by which they conceive. Women are earth-bound, seducing men with earthly desires and goods: Euridice is concupiscence; Circe is the opulence of earthly things. Helen is also terrestrial opulence, made subject at first to virtue (Menelaus), then carried off by sensuousness (Paris). When opulence marries sensuousness, vices attack the body (the Greeks attack Troy). Virtue, however, mortifies sense (Menelaus kills Paris) and then Helen gives herself to fear (Deiphobus). The celebration of Bacchus is led by Helen because opulence encourages intoxication; she leads the Trojan women, who are carnal and weak. Helen removes her lover's arms

[7] For a study of the Orpheus Legend in various classical and medieval stages, see John Friedman, *Orpheus in the Middle Ages* (Cambridge: Harvard University Press, 1970).

[8] John's commentary is given in the *Policraticus*, VIII, xxiv.

(opulence obstructs the exercise of mental powers) and invites Menelaus to kill Deiphobus, thinking she (opulence) can satisfy Menelaus
(virtue), but he is disgusted at her liason with Deiphobus (fear).

Faithful wives are considered in a different light from other
women. Commenting on adultery, Bernard says "we take women to
stand for all duty; we are taught that no one ought to lack a woman
because we all ought to impose some duty on ourselves; men who neglect their wives and pursue others abandon their duty." (This
presents an interesting analogy with romance themes.) Creusa, Aeneas' wife, is "creating use," or concupiscence in a good sense, the
power of one's search for good which is naturally united with the
human spirit. Together they produce Ascanius, whose name means
"without gradation" (*a* + *scalene*), the mean or the appropriate, without defect or excess. In other words, the product of their marriage is
the harmony of the individual, all parts in perfect balance. Creusa
plays a small part in the story, however, and since Bernard did not get
beyond Book VI in his commentary, we do not know what he might
have said of Lavinia. Fulgentius and John of Salisbury see Lavinia as
a part of Aeneas' destiny and duty: Fulgentius calls her "laborum
viam," the road of labors; John couples her with Italy, calling them
the citadel of beatitude (Pol. VIII, 24). The *Ovide moralisé* makes the
story of the *Aeneid* a religious allegory, with Aeneas as Christ or the
church, Dido as heresy, and Lavinia as the Gentiles or penitance; she
is the wife each man should take, born of his body (probably a reference to Eve), the friend without which the soul cannot have perfect
life.

In Bernard's commentary, as far as it goes, the figure who
seems to suggest the strongest contrast or counter to Dido is the Sibyl,
Deiphobe (fear of God), who leads him in the right direction. When
Aeneas is driven to the cave with Dido by storms and rain, we are told
he is led to uncleanness of flesh and lust by an abundance of humors,
the result of a superfluity of food and drink. It is called a cave because
lust obscures the clarity of mind. On his journey to the underworld,
Aeneas is guided by the Sibyl, who represents intelligence, the com-

prehension of divine things, and universal dread. She dwells in a cave, a symbol of the profundity of philosophy, secret, because it is still unknown to Aeneas, vast, because unexhausted. The cave, we are told later, is the depth of mind. The Sibyl rages because study, the violent application of mind, is like madness; she predicts because the intelligence predicts future wars against vices to prepare the spirit that is moving towards wisdom and virtue. It seems likely that Bernard means us to contrast Aeneas' two visits to a cave and to see the superiority of the second one.

In classical, as in biblical exegesis, women generally represent the weaker side of human nature. There are exceptions: the figure of Minerva, almost asexual by virtue of her birth and behavior, and the cosmological interpretations. But in the moral commentaries there is little variation. Women are lust, concupiscence, self-indulgence. One might say that the attitude towards women depends to some extent on the genre: in commentary, the interpretation of existing narratives, whether biblical or classical fiction, women are treated for the most part as evil or dangerous; in allegory, where they personify abstractions, they can represent the highest forces for good (see Chapter Two).

Index